Winning Back Life:
A Journey Through Madness and Voice Hearing

Chance Love

Copyright © 2020 David Watson

All rights reserved.

ISBN: **9798601741934**

DEDICATION

This work is dedicated to all the people that go through human experiences and believe themselves to be going mad because they were not guided, educated, or made aware of the vast extremes of the human condition.

CONTENTS

	Acknowledgments	i
1	Visions and Dreams in Youth	1
2	Growing Up	6
3	Graduating and Starting Out	11
4	Side Effects of Marijuana	14
5	Living in Rhode Island	16
6	Commands and Voices	23
7	A Little About Sexuality	25
8	The Main Players	29
9	LSD	37
10	Ventures and Misadventures	40
11	Can't Get Out	43
12	Violent and Disgusting Thoughts	50
13	Backing Up a Bit	53
14	Birthday Blues	55
15	Women	60
16	More Substance Abuse and Experimentation	62
17	Running Away from The Music Festival	69
18	I Didn't Learn My Lesson	73
19	A Nitrous Oxide Aside	76
20	Leaving for a While	78
21	Commands Are Back	82
22	Stones and Spiritual Technologies	86

23	My First Psych Ward	91
24	Back on the Road	95
25	My Second Trip Across the Country	98
26	Some More Memories of Tripping	104
27	An Uncertain Period	106
28	Processing A New Reality	112
29	Back in the Reality of Family	115
30	Retelling as "We"	118
31	New Hampshire	121
32	Living with the Boiling Undercurrent	126
33	To the Hospital!	131
34	Alone	133
35	Awareness	136
36	Medication Management	138
37	Back to Work	140
38	Processing Life by Sharing	142
39	Trying to Stop Medicating	145
40	Engaging My Mental Health	151
41	Counseling	154
42	Journaling	157
43	Career?	159
44	A Hiccup	161
45	Our Identity Experiment	163
46	The "We" Hiccup	165
47	Going to the Hospital for a Reality Check	167

48	Reaching Out	174
49	Diagnosis?	176
50	Trauma	178
51	Recovery	181
	About the Author	184

Chance Love

ACKNOWLEDGMENTS

We have to thank so many people, beings, and places for the courage to write this book and the acceptance to face our circumstances. Life has been an amazing journey full of twists and turns, fear and learning, darkness and illumination. We would like to thank the many characters met along the way. This book is really for any being who would like to better get to know what acceptance and honesty do for the confines of the human mind when it has been shut away for too long and how acceptance can burst into brilliance.

We would like to thank my parents and family for giving me shelter and letting me heal. We would like to thank the doctors and nurses from all over the country who took care of me. We would like to exclaim our love for our best friends Charles and Dan for accepting us despite our quirks and Dan, Laura, and Lily for letting us feel like we could participate with a loving family.

We met angels in strangers who offered their kindness and spirits who offered their wisdom and guidance. There are friends we haven't spoken to in years who are forever written into our lives. They always made us want to follow a path of love and find the way to live intentionally.

We would like to thank our therapists, Amy and Lorrain, for their support and sense of discovery and curiosity for our story, which has helped reignite our own. We would also like to thank the countless actors, producers, artists, singers, instrumentalists, conductors, programmers, companies, and people behind the scenes who have made countless synchronicities possible because of the exposure to their talents and art. We would like to thank all the people who work every day and keep society and the world spinning, doing jobs that they hate so that they can survive another day. We admire your constant struggle to live in this world and deal with all the difficult circumstances in life whether it is faced with anger or grace.

We are thankful for all those who cope with illnesses and their circumstances and still have hope for a better world and live day after day courageously. Finally, we would like to thank all the healers in the world who work to spread love, knowledge, tolerance, and acceptance. Every being inspires us to live selflessly.

Chance is a regular Joe like you and me. He went through hell to get the information he is sharing with you. Please take it. This is all he wants (Ivan S., my wise Hungarian friend).

1 VISIONS AND DREAMS IN YOUTH

When I was young I had a series of experiences that have weaved meaning in and out of the rest of my life. These are some but not all of the mysterious events that happened to me. There were many experiences, some that I have not described here completely, which foretold a future that I have witnessed unravel around me. The continuity of different narratives in my life have given me a partial picture of who and what I am as a human being. In telling this story I hope to share my narrative in order to see a greater reflection of my part in this world.

As a living being I have experienced wonder, awe, boredom, indifference, terror, and the gambit of thoughts, feelings, and emotions in-between. Like other human beings, the events that most affected my life were traumatic. It just was not clear to me until after I began writing that I shared more in common with other beings than I thought. My experiences were not just my own and therefore should be shared freely. Here is my story. It starts with what I recall transpiring in my youth. Some memories have always been with me, others have bubbled up more recently, from the depths, as I have begun accepting what has happened to me as the sign of a very human narrative.

A dream that I had about being a child, or an actually experience, —I don't know which:

I remember sitting down to breakfast with my mother in a kitchen that I am not familiar with. (I don't really recall much from where I lived for the first three years of life or so.) I sat at a table, and my mother was serving breakfast. I was about to eat when a voice told me not to eat the cereal, and but I started eating the cereal anyway.

When I was between 6 six and 9 nine—I don't know when, —not a

dream:

I was in my room, and I was sitting at my desk, doing something menial. All of the a sudden, a voice came out of nowhere and said to me something along the lines of "You make up the rules now." and I thought to myself that, *Wow! I get to make the rules for the world*. I don't remember exactly what I thought, but the gist was that I tried to make up a first rule. I had to think about it and paused, and then I stumbled and faltered. Then the voice basically said, "Never mind," and I never heard it again to my recollection. Still to this day, I believe that it was the all started that day when some being started me down a path to toying with rules and the need for definition in life. I hadn't told anybody about that experience for most of my adult life, and I regret that I kept it a secret, because I basically kept these and similar events to myself and they festered.

When I was very young sleeping in my bed in Connecticut:

I don't recall what I was dreaming, but I kind of woke up to the extra sensory perception of a massive machine floating above my head, one with many gears or dials that were spinning out of control. I could not understand if I was controlling it or it was controlling me. Again, I kept this experience to myself.

Many times, a reoccurring dream in my youth:

When I was younger, I had a recurring dream that I was in a very colorful world with other children, and I would hear a piercing sound, and then everybody would remain quite still, and a light would flash, and something ethereal would happen. I don't know the significance of this dream only that one time I saw an older woman with a very fancy face mask that looked like something lady Gaga would wear. Then the dreams ended when I ended up moving while I heard the piercing sound. I wasn't supposed to; and when I moved, it was like everything in that world disintegrated into chaos, pain, and yelling. I woke up confused.

When I was very young— I don't recall what age:

I was having a dream, and I woke up while dreaming, saying to myself, *"No, don't leave me!"* It was like some joyous integral part of me was stripped from me and whisked away. I remember the feeling of loss very vividly to this day, and I feel as if a part of me was either taken away or lost. I actually saw a green glowing object float away in my mind's eye.

A strange waking experience when I was younger:

I don't know what I was doing in my room, but I was sitting on my bed, and something gave me the impression that I had to stop breathing. I don't remember hearing a voice, just having the sense that I should stop breathing. So, I held my breath, and I held it and held it and held it. I was like in a trance, which, all of the sudden, I gained awareness over. When I realized that some force was influencing me to do this, I got scared and breathed. I had the sense that I was being tested for some greater purpose and had failed. This day will always haunt me because I don't recall after all these years what the purpose behind it was, but it wouldn't be the last time I tried to stop breathing.

Waking visions with voices and wise men:
I was sitting in my family room and I was alone. I can't recall if the television was on but suddenly I sensed a presence. I saw what appeared to be a large contingent of wise men wearing elaborate traditional and futuristic garments hover above me. One said "Show us you can meditate". Without thinking I acknowledged them and said "Sure!". I figured I could meditate, so I started to clear my mind and sit while focusing on nothing. I lasted about thirty seconds before a thought popped into my head. I tried again and again but kept having thoughts pop up. So, I told the wise men "I'll do it later… there's plenty of time". I was young and didn't consider what I was saying or the implications of the discipline and effort it would take to perform like these wise men may want.

The vision faded and I was alone again. Then some disembodied voices started talking to me. They told me that I could have the wisdom that the wise men offered but I had to face the worst the most painful experience of my life. The voices continued that I could go through the most awful pain or not feel a thing. In my naivety I immediately told them I would go the painless way. They disappeared at that point, but then I started to question if I made the right decision. I was only a young child and once again did not even have the implications of what I was agreeing to or not on my radar

The snow plough dreams:
After the vision of the wise men I started to have rather disturbing dreams. I called them the snow plough dreams because they seemed to happen early in the morning when I slept in on snowy days and could hear garbage trucks and snow ploughs going by. I recall that upon waking from these dreams I often was confused by their content. The dreams consisted of competitions to the death between myself and a number of other creatures and beings in the dream realm. I had to slaughter and murder my way through the dream in graphic displays of violence that I could only remember traces of when I awoke. I recall waking from these dreams feeling confused, disturbed, and detached like something significant had happened. Then the dreams would fade into waking life and their meaning would disintegrate into the ether from where they came until I started recollecting them later in life.

The ghost in the machine when I was twelve or thirteen:
This may be me combining two experiences; but even if they were two distinct experiences, the significance is still there. I was again sitting at my desk doing something. And I thought about the quote the ghost in the machine, and I realized that was a metaphor for God' existence. Basically, we live in a biological- and mechanical- based society that has a ghost that inhabits it and does all kinds of mystical and mythical stuff. I simplified it to meaning God in the Christian sense instead of just spirits or beings or entities, which would color my view for many years to come.

The other part of the experience here was not necessarily linked with this revelation; but all of a sudden, my perception shifted. It felt as if my eyes were sliding like in a slot sideways, and reality was divided into four quadrants in front of me. I don't know why I experienced this. All I know is that it was like my body took on some mechanical properties, and I was able to perceive the world through a lens, which had very strange divisions. I know I shifted these quadrants, and I altered my eyes; but to this day, I don't recall how or why. I don't know if it had any trace of an effect on me other than the memory itself.

Again, I don't remember the age but this struck me as one of the more significant mystical experiences I had experienced in my youth.
I was in my living room with family. I don't recall what we were doing, but I remember vaguely having my consciousness separate from my body. It was picked up and danced around the room with conversations from family or others around me. It seemed like a dance that was whisking me away. As I was moving around through space, somehow, I started to notice the pattern of the process that was taking place. As soon as I noticed the pattern, it was like I had achieved some type of self-awareness that took me out of step with the rest of the dance.

I wanted to dance with the movement, but I was also fascinated by the process underlying it, and so I started to falter because I was distracted from the moment and then was plunged back into my body. I was dumbstruck. I didn't know what had just happened, but I felt like I had missed another opportunity of some kind. I didn't understand then, but it would be the first of many experiences where I would become self-aware and self-conscious in a type of collective movement.

Again, I don't remember how old I was, just where I was and what happened. I was younger, and again I heard voices.:
In this case, I don't remember the circumstances again; but I was alone in my family room, and a voice came to me and started talking to me. I don't recall the gist of what it said, but I engaged it in a friendly manner;

and for whatever reason, it told me that it was time to leave. It wanted me to leave the house and go outside. It did not explain why, and so I refused to go. And that was about the time where I realized I could tell it what to do instead of it telling me what to do. I started to talk to it and tell it to do things. (I don't recall specifics.). I just know that it started vibrating very quickly like it was angry, and I eventually stopped hearing it, and it seemed to go away.

This was the first time a voice had commanded me to do something and I refused. I still don't know if the voice just wanted me to go out for an hour or a day or on a journey for the rest of my life. Either way, I found the voice to be secretive, and I felt as though it could have explained why or what it wanted me to do it. At the time, it seemed ridiculous to set off into the world on my own to live my life into what I thought would amount to a runaway when I didn't have a reason to leave, and so I did not go.

2 GROWING UP

I was a very happy child. I was very cautious at first, but also precocious and curious. I was the youngest of three children. I have a brother and a sister, who both did very well in school and have what are considered very successful careers. They make good money and work hard and smart for it.

I grew up living with my grandmother, father, mother, sister, and brother. I had a lot of love, and there was always somebody around. I lived in a house where I had some privacy, but I lived on the first floor of a two-story house; so, I was always close by the family room kitchen, and dining room. I was always within earshot, and you could hear everything in my house. I was raised in the Roman Catholic Church. I went to public school and performed very well through fifth grade. Then I went to middle school, got mixed into all new classes, and decided to be cool, which included the beginning of a lot of daydreaming and slacking, which was a waste in retrospect. I did well enough in school to stay near the top of my class, and I started as an altar boy in either fifth or sixth grade.

My experiences in church were generally those of boredom and skepticism. I went to CCD into my childhood and teenage years to learn about being Catholic, but it just seemed like a waste to me. It was like they were constantly trying to convince me that I should participate and sing and pray, but my heart was just not really in it. I prayed but not because I had faith, but because I was told to and it seemed like everybody else did it. As I got older, I continued as an altar boy and served every couple of weeks. Occasionally, I would work a wedding and get a few bucks, which was nice. But I increasingly was not seeing eye to eye with the message my priest was conveying. He was constantly going on and on about how God and Jesus are love and Jesus made this big sacrifice for everybody; and even though it was two thousand years ago, it didn't seem like anything important had really been celebrated since. In my personal life, I really didn't see God at work, especially in school.

At first in middle school, I had a few friends that I would hang out with, but I wasn't popular or anything. Luckily, in eighth grade, I was put with a new group of students and met my friends which I would continue with for the rest of high school and some college. When I got to high school, I did well, I made friends, I lusted after many girls and missed the obvious signs that many girls were lusting after me, and I generally became more concerned with society, music, and what was going on in the world.

I had a great music teacher who taught chorus. In retrospect, it had one of the largest impacts on me as far as meeting a person with a true passion for something. He introduced our class to new methods of reading music, warming up with massages and fun exercises; and he got me out of my comfort zone a lot. Unfortunately, he got really upset a lot that every person in chorus wasn't always performing to their utmost potential, and I slowly started to feel as if he was too hard on us. But the truth is now I wish more people I met in life were as passionate about what they did in life and performance as he was. Now I feel like I am as critical of others as he was because I find that your average person does not always share my passion for constructive change and positivity. I am realizing more and more that the best way to change the world is to live passionately and to help others live up to their potential. Just like what my teacher was doing.

The older I got, the more depressed I got about girls, —and I do mean girls. They were on the cusp of being women, but they still seemed just as naïve as I was. I will explain more about that later.

I also really wasn't having it with church. I got my confirmation in conformist fashion. Most of what I did at church was stare behind the altar where there was a huge stone wall. I would stare at the stones and see if I could see faces. I remember constantly thinking that if a stone morphed or changed when I was looking, I would get that sign that God was listening to me. I pretty much started prompting God to change stones so that I could get the sign that he existed. I also stared at the cross and tried to catch the enormous carving of Jesus on the cross moving.

I had my doubts, and they were getting more elaborate thanks to a sermon by my priest. This priest was truly dedicated to his job, and I am sure that for a lot of people he was preaching wonderfully, but I lost all faith during one of his children's sermons on Christmas day.

He called the children in the congregation up to the altar where they all crowded around him. Then he proceeded to start his sermon with "The presents you got this morning under your Christmas tree were not from your parents. No, they were from Jesus.". The fact that he discredited parent's' hard work and stress did not make any obvious shockwaves in the audience, but I felt my heart sink, and I decided that this church thing was really not for me.

I was amazed that he was brainwashing these children with such deceit, and it made me reflect further on how I had never gotten that sign from God or Jesus that he was there. I didn't even associate or remember any of the strange experiences that I had when I was younger because I didn't really associate them with anything the church had professed as God's body of work. I mean they resembled nothing that I had experienced outside of dreaming through sleep. It made me wish I had been aware that my experiences could have been significant. Instead, I forgot them for a time; but they were always buried there, waiting to be recalled.

After high school and some dramatics with girls, I decided I would go to UCONN because it was the cheapest school that I got into and the closest to home. I would study civil engineering because I didn't want to be like my father or my brother (they were electrical engineers), but my sister had gotten her degree in civil engineering; so, I figured why the hell, I'll try civil engineering.

Recently, the last class that I took in my master's degree in clinical mental health (big surprise), was career counseling. In this class, I learned a little about what career counselors do and how the profession has developed all types of assessments that can look at your personality, education, and interests and point you in a direction that could be more fitting to your career. Well, I had never heard of that, and I had devised no reason to talk to my school counselor; so I missed out on pursuing things like music, which I had a talent for, or art, or getting into psychology or many of the other options that I had other than engineering.

Don't get me wrong. I don't have anything against engineering. I just don't have a passion for it or the classes I took when pursuing it. Basically, I took a lot of math and physics and learned about the properties of concrete and steel and water. (I did enjoy the class on hydraulics.). I learned some cool laws of the physical universe, but I basically didn't go to class unless I had to, and I learned everything from the books for the most part. I didn't actually feel involved until my senior year when I had a project where we actually designed something. Naturally, when we logged the time applied to the final project, I ended up logging twice the number of hours in the project than anybody else in my design group.

Now the other aspect of college that I took part in was the slacking, drinking, and the real beginning of smoking pot. I started drinking in high school, but I didn't get high for the first time until college, and I had a lot of fun with it. I had nights where I would laugh uncontrollably for hours just because I smoked a few puffs of a dried herb. I felt good when I smoked, so I kept doing it when I could afford it. I even bought my first ounce freshman year of college and coveted it for a few months. Back then marijuana wasn't quite as strong, and it delivered a great state of altered consciousness. When I smoked sometimes, I found it hard to sleep; and I remember sitting up many nights analyzing my past: how I got the way I did, and what effect my parents had on me. Really just why I was the way I was. I didn't hear any mystical voices or have any type of crazy experience until my senior year of college, and that was because of magic mushrooms.

I still remember the first time I took magic mushrooms because it was such a great altered state of consciousness. I remember first taking the mushrooms and feeling nauseous and running upstairs to the bathroom and forcing myself to throw up even though I really didn't need to that badly. It took like five minutes of sticking my finger down my throat to actually puke, which was laborious. After I threw up, I still had my first psychedelic trip where I saw geometric patterns projected on everything. I had some emotional moments with a girl who was staying with us on the couch, and I went up to the mirror upstairs and got my first lesson on the power of perception.

When I got into the upstairs bathroom, the lights were out; and I looked in the reflection and could see my face all covered in shadows. I immediately had a feeling of panic, thinking why I looked so terrible. I thought this was awful, and my thoughts started to spiral until I turned on the light. Then everything was full of wonder and possibilities. I saw the potential in that young man looking back at me. He was handsome, and he had a look of wonder on his face.

At the time, I had a hat that had the word "*navy*" on it. I don't know why I had the hat, but I read that, and I immediately thought of joining the navy and becoming an admiral. I was so positive it could happen. Wow, the power of suggestion! I ended up going back downstairs and hanging out with friends. I went to a neighbor's apartment that I rarely visited and tried to have conversation with new people. I was very excited to explore and everything seemed possible. I ended up going back to my apartment, and I experienced something very strange.

We decided to play beer pong down in the basement, and I recall starting to throw balls wildly at the opposing cups, and my friends started laughing hysterically at me, and all of a sudden, I lost all track of what time it was and where I was. I felt like it had been days since I started the drug-induced trip, but it had only really been a few hours. It was 8:00 p.m. Then I kept on yelling, "What time is it? What day is it?" and my friends just thought I was hilarious.

Now that was a lot of fun, and I got my first glimpse of fractal geometric patterns, but it was a safe and enjoyable experience. I was with people who had done mushrooms before, and I didn't know what to expect, so I got a grab bag of experiences. I also didn't experience what therapists in labs do when they have you lie down with something covering your eyes and listen to relaxing music.

In therapy there is always a trained guide there in case something goes south. In laboratory experiments with hallucinogenic therapy, it sounds to me as if you go on an inward journey, which I have never really pursued, for an entire drug-induced experience. I have taken a number of psychedelics, but I didn't know to just lie down, relax, and have a vision. I would eventually have visions, but they would be with higher doses, and I would experience visualizations I almost couldn't control.

3 GRADUATING AND STARTING OUT

When I was at the end of college, I couldn't just graduate and make things simple. In my last year at UCONN, I didn't do homework in one of my classes. I was supposed to. I just didn't hand in a lot of it. So when I was supposed to graduate, my teacher basically told me I couldn't until I handed in my semester worth of homework. I then took a semester of time living off campus in a very frugal manner where I had no responsibility but to pay bills and do about ten homework exercises.

I could have gotten a summer job, but I didn't. I could have planned for after graduation and started studying for the exam that I had to take if I wanted to use my degree in engineering, but I didn't. I just relaxed and squeaked by. I, however, did make plans with a friend of mine who was participating in a program to cultivate entrepreneurs.

He was participating with a company that essentially trained college students how to run a painting business: the sales, management, and production. Then the company provided liability insurance and legal support and took a hefty cut of the profits in return. In retrospect, my friend wasn't great at managing his painting business, but we had talked about trying to open a business together, and we had the feeling that we could do something entrepreneurial; so what the heck, I joined in with him.

After I graduated from UCONN (which cost more than $60,000 I could have started a much cooler business with that money in retrospect), I moved home to Connecticut and started my own "branch" of painting company. I started by putting flyers in mailboxes for about three months and living off credit cards and my family's goodwill. I eventually hired some workers, which had a steep learning curve, and was off to the races painting houses. It was a lesson in hard work and how people in business are trying to make money off you and with you. I essentially worked for my friend. He was my boss and got a percentage of what I made, and I did everything else. After a few months of working for myself, I was pretty hooked on the idea of continuing down the path, so my friend and I decided to move to Rhode Island and make a go of it on our own. We would split everything fifty-fifty, and nobody would be our bosses.

Toward the end of my stint as an employee of this college entrepreneurial business, I got fed up with the fact that they withheld money from me. After all, I was spending my savings to get new leads and build the business, so I started working for myself and getting paid directly as a painter. The potential astounded me. In one day, I made about $2,500 by spraying a house that was white with one coat of paint. It seemed as if I could make a great living as an entrepreneur.

We paid a deposit on an apartment in a town by the ocean (it was by the ocean, so the salt does a real job on the houses), and we moved in at the end of fall. We had a very slow and uneventful winter. Basically, I played video games, kept in bed, talked to my friend, and shopped and did chores around the apartment. In addition, we started to get leads for jobs in the spring. We were poor and craved something to work on.

When the winter was over, we started getting clients and working on houses. Just my friend and I working hard every day and doing all the labor. It was tiring but rewarding work. We made enough money to get by and slowly grow the business; and after a summer of toiling, we painted the building of Steve O.

My friend met him by wandering into his shop and drumming up conversation. He was the owner of a store on the east side of Providence. The building was on a main road, and it had a lot of character. The building was essentially across the street from a twenty-four-hour convenience store and a church. Up the road was a number of bars and restaurants without a single fast food chain. The building was also located close to the college, so there were young people everywhere. Next door was a pizzeria, and every day we worked we had to endure the smell of freshly baked pizzas, a smell I would come to know and love.

As we worked for Steve, he let us know that he had an apartment for rent upstairs. He had been unable to rent it for a while, and soon it would be a new semester of school in the fall, so he was hoping it would fly off the market. The rent was $1,400 a month, which was $500 more than we were paying across town.

I can still remember every detail of that apartment. On the second floor of the building was the door to the apartment, which was adjacent to the door to the other apartment in the building, which took up the majority of the second floor. The apartment we were offered had an odd mudroom on the second floor that eventually became our office, and then there was a stairway up to the third floor. The third floor had an open layout; and the living areas were divided by a utility closet, which separated the front living area from the kitchen and main common area.

There was one bedroom and one bathroom on the third floor, and on one side of the house the windows opened up to a 15x35 feet of flat roof, which ran the length of the building. In the front living area, there was a black wooden ladder, which went up to the master bedroom on the fourth floor. On the fourth floor, the ceiling was pitched; and on there was a long hallway down the center of the layout, which led past a large bathroom on the left, then a bedroom, and two storage rooms on the right. (One eventually became a bedroom even though it had no windows or ventilation.) At the end of the hall was a master bedroom, which was the largest bedroom in the building. It had a small closet and looked out on the neighborhood. We agreed to move in immediately.

Why was this apartment so important? What transpired here really changed the trajectory of my life. I had more drug-induced confusion, delusions, insights, victories, greed, plotting, fun, manipulation, commands from voices, contemplation, and spiritual journeys in the years of life when my brain was finalizing its major development than at any other point in my life to date. I started to search inwardly for answers to the big questions and got pointed in a new direction away from greed and wants and to necessities and love. This apartment would place me in grave danger of losing my freedom, my mind, my sanity, my very grip on reality. I would meet influential people and beings. I would become morally flexible and start to truly experiment on life itself.

4 SIDE EFFECTS OF MARIJUANA

I started smoking pot when I was in college. I was not a heavy smoker like some of my friends. I didn't rely on it to get through the day. I thought of it as a bit of fun now and again. I always had friends who smoked, and I guess peer pressure got the best of me; but as most people find out, marijuana is really a good time, and it made me think. I analyzed everything that I could when I lay in my bed after smoking. It was like I had an amazing tool to make connections that my mind never had considered before.

I really should have been studying psychology because I was basically psychoanalyzing myself whenever I smoked. The problem was that it affected my memory, and I couldn't remember a lot of the creative conclusions I had drawn; and in a lot of situations, I would talk about all kinds of ambitious ideas with friends. The next day, it was as if it didn't happen because I just could no longer recall the content of our conversations. All I had was the vague recollection of an enjoyable interesting experience which drew me further to pot.

The other side effect of marijuana that I really liked was the fact that it could make me stop worrying about the world and what the news said; and what I could see was a flawed system of government; and all the policies about everything from criminal law to the way society treated or didn't treat its homeless; and how big pharma, big tobacco, special interest groups and that people with money seemed to be in power. It all seemed unfair and stressed me out. The system I was living in really just didn't seem to be comfortable until I started smoking marijuana. My priorities changed. I started to focus less on the problems of the world and more on just the pleasures in life. Marijuana was the first step in rethinking what I thought was important in the world.

Essentially marijuana allowed me to escape the stress that perceiving the troubles of the world causes. I felt light when I smoked. Everything would just melt away and I would be present with the possibilities of the moment. I was usually smoking with friends. Smoking became a social norm and a niche community which I could rely on to feel safe. Smoking was a release, a way to not worry, and a community where it was okay to just enjoy and relax despite all the chaos and craziness that I knew was constantly happening all around me.

I believe I used marijuana to really cope with the wider world. It created a state of mind that was a refuge from our society's cruel nature. Marijuana really allowed me to forget about what stressed me out and reprogram my pursuit of the here and now. The problem was that it also messed with my memories of the here and now and the fun that existed in those high moments. There's no wonder that humans gravitate towards marijuana to deal with the grind of reality.

Marijuana also did one really life defining thing: normalize experimentation with substances. I was a D.A.R.E. kid. I watched the commercials about your brain on drugs. When I smoked marijuana, I had a harmless good time. It was not the deadly encounter with risky behavior. Everybody called marijuana the gateway drug. For me it truly was a gateway because marijuana was a drug that created fun times and relaxation, but it was vilified beyond rational recognition.

5 LIVING IN RHODE ISLAND

When I moved into the new apartment, my business partner and I started to also hire new workers in the hopes that we could shift to management positions and focus on growing the business. It was the beginning of the economic downturn, but we were hungry for work. In our new apartment we started to branch out into the community. But close to home we found a different community.

At first, we met our downstairs neighbor, a closeted pot dealer who worked at a liquor store, and his roommate Todd who would become a close friend of mine. We liked the new digs, and we slowly got used to living on the east side. I worked really hard to maintain that apartment. I would work up to thirty days straight when the weather permitted, and then I would do all kinds of side jobs at night. Our business was growing, but I was funding most of it with credit cards. My neighbors made smoking marijuana easy because it was available, acceptable, and cheap.

When we first started looking for new employees, we started interviewing locals and students for the job of painter, which paid a measly $10 or $11 an hour, and I ended up meeting a foreign girl named Marissa. She was a student at college, and I really didn't know that she could handle the work we were doing because it was very physically demanding; basically, painting took working out your arms and back for eight hours a day. But we met and had coffee together, and I decided not to hire her. She struck me as confident in herself but a little naive about the work she was trying for. I didn't really think she absolutely needed the job, and she was a student, so I really, really didn't think she needed it, but that was not the last time I saw Marissa.

After we hired some new workers, we continued grinding away with our little company. Time passed quickly as we toiled to grow our business. My relationship with my business partner fluctuated as we made and lost money. Around that time, I had a rigorous work-oriented routine. I would do hard physical labor most days and work out at night. I would spend my down time with the neighbors and started to branch out making friends with the various smokers and students that frequented my downstairs neighbor's apartment.

This period of stability lasted at least six months, but change was inevitable and new neighbors moved in downstairs. They were both students from the local college. Joseph and Nathan. Through them and keeping in contact our previous apartment mates, I started making more and more new friends. But now, I started meeting more college students; and they all seemed very liberal and open-minded, which was refreshing. And then by chance, I met Marissa again; and we became friends. At about the same time, I was looking for a way to smoke marijuana for free, so I started asking around where people got their pot. Marissa told me she had somebody I had to meet. So I went across town and met Bob.

Little did I know that Bob was a very talented artist. He could draw amazing portraits of people and monsters from his imagination. He had gone into business for himself; and somehow, he acquired two apartment buildings. He wanted to fix them up and rent them, but something disastrous happened, and the pipes froze, and there was water damage. He lost them. Then he started a porn store and ran that for some time. He knew all kinds of people, and he started selling them pot. And he found that selling pot was easier and was a lot less effort, so I think he just kind of fell into it.

Bob was a fascinating character for me. He relied on pot to make a living and he was as unique as they come. The thing about Bob was he had this very intense way of talking. He would have these long intense commentaries, and he would talk so fast and with such emotion that it made him seem like something was amiss. I liked Bob because he was honest, intense, and charismatic. He really had a point of view, and he seemed a little paranoid and angry, but that may have been because he smoked so much pot.

Bob lived in a loft apartment of a converted mill and had a great apartment with these huge rooms and a great atmosphere. He lived with his friends who were a couple and worked for a bread factory. They were perpetually high and carefree. Bob showed his paranoia by wiring up his door with a camera, but the funny thing is he took the security precautions with the camera but then pretty much let anybody into his apartment.

Bob sold me my first ounce of low-quality herb for $110. It didn't seem like a big deal at the time, just a small investment. I figured I could sell to the college kids I knew and smoke for free. It was win-win, but what if it was illegal? I took that ounce and sold it in eighths to my friends and charged them $25 an eight, which was a great price. I had the connection to

Bob, and I had a great price, and people just kept coming back to me.

Over the course of a few months I slowly built my way from my buying an ounce to a quarter pound, and then I kept saving and selling until I started buying better-quality herb for $300 to $450 an ounce, which I then sold for $60 to $70 an eighth. So I continued to network with new students and started going to college parties, and before I knew it I was looking to buy my first pound of herb. My first pound cost me something like $4,000, and I got it from a very sketchy dealer that I can't recall how I made the acquaintance. I just know I asked everybody where they got their herb, and they would just tell me and introduce me to more people.

I couldn't seem to satisfy the demand that my friends had for smoking pot. No matter what I did people started to seek me out to get more herb. Dealing was becoming a way to be important and sought after. It was easy to network with potheads. And I had a knack for finding product. I started to network with dealers and find bigger and bigger sources so that I could satisfy my customers. The money was amazing, and I was around smokers all the time, so I was smoking very casually but not too often in order to maximize my profits.

Then some strange things started to happen when I smoked. I started having thoughts like there was a game going on, and I sensed what I can only describe as trades going on. For some reason, I would find myself "making a trade" with somebody and then thinking to myself, *No, I don't want to do this*. I still don't know what was happening. There existed a narrative in my mind that I was trading away something personal to others, but the state of mind that I experienced this informational exchange only was occurring when I smoked.

I really slowed down smoking after that. I felt as though there was more going on than met the eye. It may also have been that when I was smoking pot and analyzing myself, I had started to detect the very mechanisms of consciousness, like observing the different stages of collapsing and expanding attentional states. Sometimes I would feel the network of neurons firing in my brain, and I would be able to change how I was feeling by just thinking about it. At the time these experiences did not strike me as anything but a side effect of smoking. I really did not consider the access that I was able to achieve of observing different activities of the mind and body and the different perceptual states that allowed for seeing unconscious processes at work.

I started hanging out with Marissa more, and we talked about philosophy and our problems with people. She was an artist and was an aspiring lawyer. She was from Europe and spoke with a thick accent. She told me all about how she trained ruthlessly to become a ballerina when she was younger. I secretly thought she was beautiful, but we just stayed good friends and smoked together and hung out.

Marissa became a confidant and regular. We would frequent each other's apartments and generally we hung out in similar circles of people. Over time we became closer as I opened up and we shared beliefs in reality, philosophy, and we sought out our purpose in this world. Eventually I got very comfortable around Marissa, and I didn't think twice when I got the opportunity to take psychedelic mushrooms with her.

At this point, I was making a fair amount of money selling herb. I had expanded my network and was selling to other dealers. I had met other dealers who sold herb by the pound and were trying to find connections to bigger and bigger distributors. The demand was outweighing what I could provide, and I wanted a consistent supply. Money was coming in from the pot hand over fist. It was like a spigot that I could not turn off.

At the same time, I was running my little painting company with my business partner. I began supporting it with loans from my dealings because there was a recession starting and people really didn't want work done unless it was necessary. We had a number of Spanish workers that had families which I had become greatly involved with. Since I was the production manager it was up to me to manage and interact with the workers.

I worked closely with my workers to ensure that we performed a quality service. I got to know them like family. I became close friends with workers who has their own surprising stories. Michael who I found out was actually an active gay porn star and hung out with the Mayor's boyfriend. I also became close with the work foreman, Tito, who was illegally in the country and using somebody else's passport to work for us.

My workers became dear to me. I took pride in the work we did, and I worked hard to keep the painting company producing. However, the cost of business took its effect. The painting company was not paying the bills anymore. My business partner was slowly letting me invest more and more money in the company in order to keep it running. As he continuously looked the other way at my dealing activities he kept taking unsecured loans to pay our workers.

I started to spend less and less time working on the business to the point where I was spending a lot more time actively dealing and socializing with customers. This exposed me to more and more drug culture and the younger quasi-adults that were partying and working hard to make their way in the world. The more exposed I got to drugs the more normal taking them seemed and soon I started to doubt all the lessons I had learned about the dangers of illicit substances.

On one weekend I took mushrooms with Marissa one night and went to a party. I remember sitting in the party and seeing Marissa playing with an iPod. That was the first time I saw somebody playing with a device that started to make me interactively feel sensations that I can only describe as waves of feeling. It moved through my body with the synchronicity of her playing with the buttons on her iPod. It was a pleasant energy that I could feel in a field around my body. At the time, I was tripping on mushrooms; so I didn't say anything. After the sensation had subsided, I tried to talk to other people, but I could not organize my thoughts, so I just sat at the party looking around and trying to reconcile what the experience was.

Eventually, as the party pushed towards two in the morning, I would join in and start dancing when a girl that I liked came into the room. I still had the sense that something was going on greater than myself behind the scenes. So I went outside and had a conversation with a friend, where I tried to convince him that there was more to reality. He didn't give me a direct answer that I was sensing anything out of sorts. He didn't refute it either; and in our conversation, I got the gist that he wasn't allowed to admit anything. And so, my assertions of a veiled existence persisted.

For some reason, there were a lot of magic mushrooms around; so I would go on to do them with my friends Joseph and Nathan and even my friend Tom. They would be interesting adventures where I would venture out into the world and have waves of feeling very fragile and so alive. I remember sitting by the bay in the winter and feeling vulnerable like I could feel my body dying. I had experiences where I could savor the very essence of life as a fleeting and dangerous experience.

I remember doing mushrooms with Marissa again and being in her apartment. Her cousin was over, and she had a Buddha poster in her living room. I remember looking at that Buddha poster and seeing it pulsate and shift from one Buddha to another. It just kept morphing and glowing. It was beautiful. During that mushroom trip, I went into the bedroom with Marissa and her cousin. I had the greatest desire to have a threesome I would ever have, and I got bold and took off my belt and put my arm around Marissa's cousin. I guess it didn't go so well because I didn't get lucky. Instead, I recall a few things happening.

For one thing, we started listening to music, and I found myself being so emotional and had the thought that God speaks through music. This idea never left me. Then I remember walking into the kitchen and having a waking hallucination that was like coming in and out of a blackout; I don't remember what I saw, only that when I left the kitchen, I felt as if I were in control of a video game, and I, Chance, was the player. I made myself walk into a wall, and controlling my body really felt like being a puppeteer. I had just taken control of some new and shiny toy.

I went back into the room, and Marissa was making art by dripping watercolors onto paper. It was beautiful, and I watched waiting to be invited to make art with the girls; but they never invited me, so I just observed. That's when I noticed on the paper that the little blobs of waterborne paint overlapped one another. You could see each individual drop and what form it took, but they overlapped loosely.

In that moment, I saw the abstract view of how the different artificial constructs in the world interact. They each have their organizational structure, which allowed it to adapt to new environments. Different abstract entities have a vested interest in surviving to make money or promote research or organize laws or help people or teach. Different types of organizations, from companies to government to charities, all had people propping them up, growing them, giving them purpose and the ability to grow and adapt to a changing world, and investing in making new policies to further their causes. I could see this because of the relationships I saw in the art, and it was mind-blowing to me.

I started to call it the collective conscious because I thought it existed as a result of the collective organization of people. The more I thought about it, the more I attributed lifelike qualities to the abstract organizational paradigm; and the idea eventually merged with the unconscious will of people. This creates a whole living society that is organizationally made of so many tiny parts that create larger and larger living entities, starting with energy that makes up particles, which make up elements, which make up molecules, which make up cells, which make up organs, which make up plants and animals, which make up abstract entities, which in turn grow to control and evolve as we do.

At the same gathering with Maria I also has an experience of seeing the organization of special objects through a different perceptual lens. I recall looking around her apartments and noticing a particular set of patterns in which objects were oriented. There were obvious fractal patterns in the way that spatial objects were organized. Art supplies, furniture, anything in the rooms was seen through being placed spatially in a relationship with other objects. I could see the fractal organization like trees in a forest are fractally spaced. This was an example of seeing through a perceptual lens that is our unconscious mind has access to and is normally veiled in average everyday life.

My understanding of the world was growing quickly, but I had some odd experiences again, similar to the feelings of trading. I remember being with a number of friends, and I was high on pot or so I recall. I had a conversation with the people there where I was answering a question along the lines of what you would do if you were a god and could do whatever you wanted. My response was that I would give food the attributes of pot that make you high and water would be like LSD so that everybody would be free. Keep in mind I hadn't tried LSD yet, but somehow that experience always stuck with me because it seemed significant that I thought that.

I also had many late nights where I experienced what I can only describe as a feeling that the world had ended. I was looking up in my apartment, and I saw a strange combination of colors, and then I had the sense that everything reset around me like I was living in the matrix. This is another experience that has stuck with me. Over and over I experienced the feeling like reality had ended and everything that I experienced was newly reformed. It was like being in a faulty video game that was crashing, and it was an experience I observed but did not share.

When I was on psychedelics I had numerous ideas and epiphanies about how to live differently and authentically. I made dozens of connections in my mind about who to network with and alternative ways of doing business. But for some reason I didn't think to speak directly of my experiences with other people. It was like on some level I was just accepting what was happening to me as normal and then packing them away. In a sense I was not acknowledging the gifts I was being given in the form of experiences and exposure to what is possible to humanly live.

Now when I look back and reflect on those times and the confidence I had in the people that I had connected with. Unfortunately, I was sowing the seeds of uncertainty about my beliefs around that point. I was just starting to openly question reality around me. Despite my early childhood experiences, it is as if I was indoctrinated to belief that magic and spirit did not exist. Religion didn't pan out and I was living without a compass to guide me or an anchor to keep me grounded.

My friends and I were normalizing experimentation with substances with no formal training or thought of what the consequences of using substances would be. I was naïve, but my eyes have been opened since enough times to see that substance use deserves respect. Education and guidance about the substance use and its' spiritual, mental, and physical consequences are lacking in this day in age for your average person looking to escape from today's stressful world.

Recognizing that substances allow people to escape or transcend everyday life is important. But recognizing that what we are escaping to with substances may change us for life in unpredictable ways without proper preparation, guidance, and education are even more important.

Additionally, the people I were meeting seemed interesting and new. Everybody was so into me because I had what they needed. I was networking and making friends as I had always done, but now my friendships were beginning to be tied to dealing. I was infatuated with being the center of attention of so many people. It was exciting to go from the lonely life of working like a dog for seventy hours a week to hanging out with group after group of enthusiastic beautiful people. The popularity felt amazing. I felt like I had friends again, but my relationships were caught in the gravity of my dealing endeavors.

6 COMMANDS AND VOICES

Now we come to the first time I heard a command from a voice while smoking pot. Naturally, I was alone after smoking with friends, and I was on my couch. All a sudden, I heard from a robotic-sounding voice, "Go outside and run around naked." Now I didn't think of this as abnormal. I just accepted that there was a disembodied voice talking to me. It seemed like out of the blue and on some level, it must have felt familiar to me. But my reaction was basically not to do that. I thought to myself it was too much trouble to follow the voices command, so I figured I would do it later or some other time.

Then the voice repeated itself. That is when I started to think to myself, *Why?* and *What is this voice?* I started to question the voice. I started asking it why and what it was, and it basically told me in very rudimentary terms that it would not tell me anything and that I should do what it told me. The irony here is that if I had listened to the voice, I would have probably been arrested and possibly admitted to a mental ward where I could have been treated and perhaps disinclined to continue smoking and whatnot. Instead, I started to mess with the voice.

Somehow, I subvocalized something in my throat and the voice said what I had subvocalized. That is when I should have realized that the voice was partially mine and it was connected to me in some fashion, but I was not analyzing at this point. I was in the mood to experiment. I started to use my ability to subvocalize and manipulate the voice to make the voice talk to me and have conversation against the voice's will.

It told me to stop messing with it, and I didn't listen. As I continued, I could hear another robotic voice in another pitch chime in. And I started asking it questions. It didn't really give me the answers I wanted, and then I heard another pitched voice and another, and I found that there were multiple voices each with different pitches that could talk to me and that I could control by sub vocalization. Not only that, but after I started to manipulate the voices by putting words in their voices, I could also hear them (sometimes very faintly) talking to one another. This only got me more intrigued. Now this experience didn't last forever, just until my high wore off and I got to my sober state of consciousness. Afterward, I just kind of went on my way like nothing had happened. I kind of forgot about the experience after it happened. I unintendedly kept the fact that I heard voices to myself, which potentially was a mistake.

I also had one other experience while high on pot that's worth mentioning. Again, when I was alone in my apartment, I don't recall what I was doing; but I got the sense that something was leaving me in a similar fashion to when I was young and had dreamed a part of me was leaving. I could sense other beings were leaving this realm and I was convinced that I was a part of their group. This time, however, I was told that if I stopped breathing, I could come with them. I don't recall if it was a robotic voice, but anyhow I lay down on the ground and held my breath. Basically, I just kept holding my breath and holding my breath.

As the feeling that I needed to breathe swept over me, I found that it didn't really bother me because I was so detached by the herb. I kept laying there expecting something to happen, but nothing did. After a few minutes of ignoring my need to breath easily, a doubt crept into my mind. This was a very human doubt, something along the lines of what if they are tricking you and you will just die? Now this really messed with me. The doubt made me waiver, and I lost my gumption. I started to breathe. I was terribly conflicted and got the sense that I missed out on something epic; so, I lay there in indecision, trying to stop breathing and then letting doubt sabotage me. This is another event in my life where I doubt I would have died, but I may have experiences something "other." This was not the last time I would hold my breath.

These experiences strike me as important because I really did not think that what was happening was bizarre. Instead because I was high and carefree at the times when these events happened. Because I did not have any comprehension of the significance of hearing voices in practice I found the experience intriguing. On some level I didn't think what was happening was worth mentioning to others because I wasn't sure of what the response would be. What would other people think about hearing voices or being able to stop breathing? These events did not fit into the framework of my normal life and therefore they did not hold my attention for what they were revealing. Something significant was afoot. A story larger than me was making its way into my life.

7 A LITTLE ABOUT SEXUALITY

When I was a child, I had a neighbor. When he moved in, our houses we back to back; so we started hanging out because of affinity to each other. I was maybe five at the time, and we would hang out after church. One time in particular, we were hanging out in his basement. We ended up starting to strip and get naked and dance around together. I don't recall feeling like we were being so much sexual as expressing our freedom after going to church. We danced around playfully naked, and it was innocent.

Then another time we raided his sister's underwear drawer, stole some thongs (which was amazing because she was only a few years older than us and already wearing thongs before she hit puberty, I don't remember exactly how old I was at this point, but I don't think I was that much older), and then my friend proceeded to put one on. I don't recall trying one on, but I may have.

Another item of note that I experienced with this young friend was that I saw breasts for the first time with him. We were watching Police Academy part one, which was rated R. We were technically too young to watch it, but my friend's parents were relaxed. There was a scene on the beach where this girl took off her bathing suit top at a bonfire and danced around. I don't have a memory of her naked breasts; instead, I have a memory of watching the movie again on TV and seeing the same scene with this woman having been edited so she is dancing behind the flames but you cannot see her nakedness.

I had another experience when I was younger, at around the age of five, with another neighbor, the first girl I really "liked." We hung out all the time because she lived down the road from me. We played soccer together, and she was pretty good. We hung out all the time and played games; and once—just once—we played doctor under her ping-pong table. We built a fort over the table by draping colorful blankets over the sides. Then when we were underneath the table, Julie proceeded to check me out like a doctor. I had to take off my shirt, and she checked my heartbeat. Then she said, "Drop your pants," and I took off my pants and underwear. I don't remember anything sexual about the experience, but then it was my turn to be doctor, and she wouldn't take off her clothes. I just know I felt gypped because at the time I knew we were different sexually, but I had never seen the private parts of a girl.

Anyhow, I lived in a Roman Catholic family where sexuality was repressed. I was not ever given a clue about sexuality from my parents. I remember seeing mother and father naked at a particularly young age, and I have some vague recollections of being breastfed; but beyond that, I really got no cues as to what the norm was. When I got interested in masturbating for the first time, I went on the Internet to look up pictures of women.

Now keep in mind that again I lived on the first floor of my open-floor house, and I never would shut my door. On top of which, the Internet was in its infancy so that download speeds were prehistorically slow. There were so few provocative sites that the best way to find them was by using the directories feature on Yahoo. That's right—an Internet directory like the phonebook, only for risqué topics—and after you clicked a link, the link changed color, and there was evidence that you had browsed it. (This made me paranoid.)

Then I went online and somehow found a picture of a partially naked woman, and I started to go to business with my penis. I didn't really know what to expect, so I just kept things moving, and I started to feel weird but in a good way. It felt like I was building toward something, but I persisted through the weird feeling I was getting. And after confronting a threshold that seemed unsurmountable, bam, I came for the first time and had a wonderful pleasant sensation.

I couldn't help but think that was so cool. Like where was this in my life. The next day I carefully and secretly went online again. (The amazing thing is that I had a computer at this point in my life with an ancient processor and Windows 95.) I carefully listened to make sure nobody was on my side of the house; then in secret, I found another picture of a woman. I started to go to the business of manipulating myself. This time, however, I was in a hurry, so I tried to cum faster so that I could get the same feeling but more quickly. Big mistake: I got what I wanted, which was a really pathetic premature orgasm. I would try again and again to get back to that first type of experience, but I wouldn't really be able to until I was about twenty-seven and with a girl named Amanda, whom I felt relaxed around and took my sweet time with.

For a long time, I was sexually frustrated by masturbation, and I think it had an effect on how I interacted with girls. For one thing, I used porn and physical beauty as a moniker for what I desired in woman sexually; on the other hand, I tended to admire a woman from a distance in my own head and built them up before talking to them, always with some fear of rejection or the feeling that I may be "discovered."

I had incredibly high standards of physical beauty for women, which was unfortunate because I know for a fact that I overlooked a number of very beautiful girls while looking for those with the most mature bodies that lived up to an image of beauty reminiscent of models—and fully physically developed women at that. The funny thing is that I didn't even understand what I was doing; essentially, I was rejecting what was right in front of me for an ideal. (That behavior plays largely in the role of why I ended up with a diagnosis of schizophrenia.)

I learned to ruminate over these girls and construct wild fantasies of what I would say to them and how we could be together and what it would be like to date them. It was an exercise in intellectual masturbation; and I wish I just had learned to walk up to girls, get to know them, then date them to find out if I was sexually attracted to them for who they were. It's the healthy way.

I would like to think I am attractive; in middle school and high school, I got attention from so many girls who liked me, but I really missed out because of my standards and the delusions I had about who was worthy of desire. The truth was that the girls that I was after would probably just make me have a premature ejaculation. When I took my time later in life and slept with Amanda, I had great orgasms. I had met her while trying to get with a girl that I found out had a boyfriend; and in my drunken disappointment, I settled for Amanda who was really into me.

The more I hung out with Amanda, the more I liked her and the better the sex got. What I should have been taught at a young age is that sexuality, especially masturbation, is about reaching a climax in a relaxed setting where you don't have to worry about anything but the experience. As I grew older, I wish I was taught that it is not always what society deems beautiful that you should believe is beautiful. I wish I had dated all those girls who were interested in me and gotten some real experience with dating women. Instead, subsequently, I dated women very sparsely; and relationships didn't really last long because when I was in love, things didn't play out cleanly. When I threw my hat in the ring, I just didn't find "the one."

I bring my sexuality up now because it generally has not been expressed to the degree that I or many others hoped that it would be in life. In Rhode Island despite my constant networking and mingling with men and women, I wasn't really getting into relationships. On one hand I wanted to have sex, on the other hand I couldn't see a lasting future with a woman if drugs were involved. So, throughout my time in Rhode Island I remained in a sexually limbo for most of the time.

I had relationships very infrequently and I believe I was impacted by the risks that I was willing to take with the law. Since I was unattached for most of the time, I tended to play it fast and loose. I didn't need to worry about the consequences of my actions and the romantic ramifications of being pinched for most of my time as a dealer. But when I did get into relationships with women the dealing always messed with my identity and subsequently what I saw was possible for my relationship's future.

8 THE MAIN PLAYERS

Back by the ocean, I met many colorful people who played prominent roles in my future delusions, which were fueled by a steady stream of psychedelic experiences and out-of-the box thinking while exposing myself to new belief systems like reiki and acupuncture, the secret, classic mythology, the idea that dreams were a path to self-understanding, and even astrology, which I view as a sort of psychic placebo.

I met Brian, an overachiever disguised as a slacker, who was a true poet, a musician, a philosopher, a pothead, and who I would consider my most interesting friend. We would smoke pot with friends and talk about philosophy and how to actualize our desires and manifest them in the world. We hung out often; and as I got to know him, he was getting his shit together. He went to community college and eventually worked his way to Columbia University. I have tried to get back in touch with him, but he has not been as forthcoming as I hoped.

There was Todd, a positive and interesting individual who was my best friend at one point. He took adventures to Spain and tried to live there for a few months without any luck. He ended up moving in with me and working for me for the summer where he saved enough money to move out to California to get away from Rhode Island. He found happiness out there, and I recently talked to him and found out he was married and his fortune continues to grow.

Nathan and Joseph were my downstairs neighbors after Todd moved out the first time. They were students at college and helped introduce me to all kinds of people. Nathan was a charismatic, beautiful man who could charm the pants off anybody with a smile. He would go on to become a doctor and father with a woman he met at Burning Man. Joseph was an amazingly involved advocate for the use of medical marijuana. He was inspirational to me that he could work the system and effectively change the laws in Rhode Island to allow patients to ingest marijuana legally. Joseph looked frail but had such ambition and drive that he could make true change even though at the time he could barely cook pasta. We were fast friends; and after he graduated from college, he moved to California, and so did Nathan. Joseph got his law degree; and as far as I can tell, he is continuing his advocacy efforts. He had perpetual trouble with girls in Rhode Island, but he met his wife in California.

I met Rick through Bob. Rick was an ex-meth addict who sold and smoked pot medicinally because he hadn't found a better way to self-medicate. He was a swinging, open-minded, free spirit that I loved truly and dearly. Despite his years of use, he was generally a jovial person; he had a boyfriend and was eventually interested in the same woman I was. I saw Rick as a guide of sorts to a hippie-like existence. It was him I called when I was having a bad trip; he gave me helpful and scary advice. I saw him as a godly spirit and as a very tired old soul at times when I was tripping. I became somewhat obsessed with him and a few other people and how they fit into my life but more on that later.

Harry was another charismatic hippie with a long beard, a deep loud voice, and not an ounce of shame to spare. I met him because he knew how to grow plants, which he would eventually grow for me. He also dealt to make money, and he would be one of my go-to guys. I was always trying to give him advice and be positive around him. It was like sometimes he couldn't get out of his own way. Harry was eccentric; he lived on the edge of society and had no fear when it came to doing what needed to get done, like driving across town on a snowy night on a scooter with weight strapped to his back. He was hilarious, jovial, and incredibly entertaining; and he smoked like a chimney.

Steve O was my landlord. He was a very experienced older gay man. He was very open about who he was and what he wanted from the get go of meeting him. He was perpetually interested in my sex life. He more or less gave me the open invitation to experiment with him and his partner if I would like without much pressure. He became a confidant about what was going on in my life and business, but I kept the involvement with drugs from him. I kept the psychedelics, delusions, and extrasensory experiences including voices to myself. He remarked to me on more than one occasion that he didn't think everything was all right with me and that I had options to get help, but I wasn't interested in listening because I felt I was in the middle of some grand experiment.

I met Michael because I painted his house, and we hit it off over talk of video games. He was the manager where he worked, and he got to where he was through hard work. He had waited until he was older to get married, and he married a lovely woman with two grown children. Michael was a rock to me; he was like an older brother and father combined. We kept in touch and started hanging out and playing Gears of War with each other until he presented me with the opportunity to "work" for his company. After that, we met at least every two weeks; but I kept the drugs from him because he had responsibilities, and I didn't know what he would think of the liberties that I was taking.

I met Alex when he came to me looking to buy some pot. He had been robbed for a lot of money, and he was rebuilding, and I was happy to help him get back on his feet. I found that he was a master of manipulating people to his wants and needs. I don't think it was malicious. It is just what he learned. He also tried to help me when I was really falling apart mentally. I ended up living with him for a few months without a job or any real way to make money other than with pot. He took me in, and I gave him all my connections when I really wanted out of the business. He muscled me out of the game when I really couldn't mentally cope; gave me my share of the profits, which was surprisingly light compared to the money I knew he was making off my methods of dealing; and then sent me on my way.

There were many more people that had impacts on my time in Rhode Island; but at this point, it has been so long that I have talked to them that I have even forgotten some of their names. One person I cannot forget is Richard. I met Richard in college at our orientation for becoming engineers. We played Frisbee together and made fun of other kids. Then we went our separate ways after college orientation. During the first week of college, I was going back to the dorms with some girls; and I happened to meet up with a kid I had played pickup soccer with over the summer.

He invited me to hang out, and I ended up in Richard's room. I started frequenting his room that year and became a fixture. As I opened up to Richard and told him some of my vulnerabilities, I ended up getting made fun of and mocked by him and his roommate, so I basically was like "fuck that noise" and started hanging out with my neighbor in my dormitory Matt. Matt and I became best friends, and I slowly integrated him into the group that Richard and I would eventually form socially.

Richard and I stayed friends through college into becoming business partners and even after I started dealing. We argued a lot, but we had the same goal in mind to become successful. This idea kept us together until I felt as though he was no longer carrying his weight in the painting business. In effect I was supporting the business largely by dealing. Toward the end, he owed me roughly $30,000. My credit cards were pretty much maxed out to the tune of $20,000. I also had other prospects and business opportunities popping up because of all my networking. I convinced my friend Joe to venture out into a marketing business with me, and we made a little money doing educational marketing in California.

I met Daniel through selling herb. He was the most brilliant computer programmer I have met. He was a gentle soul who had his own mental issues. He had at least one mental breakdown while I knew him, and he was heavily medicated, which he hated. So he self-medicated with pot, which is where I came in to the story. Daniel told me an idea for an app that was a mobile social aggregator. Socialite would combine the functionality of a bunch of social apps and Facebook to create a social hub for the mobile phone. At the time, Facebook Mobile had not come out, and I saw the potential to make money. At first, he needed $5,000 or $6,000 to get started, and I thought no problem. I committed to him and started a small software company we incorporated in Delaware.

Daniel's father was a very successful businessman in finance in New York City, and he wanted Daniel to go into finance, but Daniel's heart was in programming. His talent was with programming, and I thought he could do things with computers that I would probably have a hard time comprehending unless I got my doctorate in computer science. Daniel's father didn't see it that way, and so Daniel convinced his father to let him take a break from college and pursue entrepreneurship. Daniel's father would mostly support him; and in return, Daniel wouldn't invest any money into the business. However, Daniel's father would pay for all the legal fees.

This endeavor with Daniel was what ended my business with Richard. I had been trying to get Richard to consider getting involved with the drugs, but he didn't want to, so I tried bringing up other business ideas with him, but he wasn't really having it.

One day I made the decision that I no longer wanted to be the production manager of a painting company. I had worked really hard to get my crew to the point where they were efficiently working without me on site. I really was working just three or four hours a day with the painting company, and I was ready to move onto something else. I basically told Richard that he could run the company and I would get involved again after he paid me back. He said he didn't want to do that and that he wanted to just take over the business himself. I loosely got him to agree to signing a loan agreement that he would pay me back $20,000. I got a lawyer to make the agreement, and he moved out. When the time came to sign the agreement, he refused.

I didn't really have any form of recourse, and so we ended up parting ways. Eventually, my friend Alex threatened Richard in an attempt to intimidate him; and after that, Richard and I have not talked at all. On some level, I felt betrayed by Richard because he let me work my ass off for our collective good. I was at the point where I no longer wanted to work 80-hour weeks between dealing and painting to scratch by. The painting company was becoming more of an expense than anything. I ended up parting with Richard after working any way I could to make ends meet for us after three long years. He just took advantage of the situation and covered his own ass.

I started working with Daniel to build the app, which I wanted to call Socialite, a few months after Joseph and Nathan moved out. Richard S. and his roommate, who I cannot recall the name of, moved in downstairs. Yes, another, Richard. Richard S. was a student from college that I did not know had a pill problem, and his roommate worked in Massachusetts as an EMT. When they lived downstairs from Richard and me, they started having parties where they would take a drug called mephedrone.

Mephedrone has a similar effect to ecstasy, and it gives you sensation of pleasure and comfort that usually leads to sexual encounters. I eventually became friends with them and got invited to their parties; but by then, I think the small group that was experimenting with this drug was feeling the effects of so many interpersonal experiences on their social lives. When I hung out with them, they would invite girls from Massachusetts, the same friends, and hang out in bathing suits and flirt with each other and have fun. I thought they were great. When Richard moved out, I convinced Richard S. and his roommate to move in with me.

This is when Daniel and I really ramped up work on Socialite. Daniel moved in downstairs; and he invited his friend Danika, another brilliant New Yorker, who could perform magic with video editing equipment and knew how to create mystical and ethereal sounds on her bass guitar. Danika was also eccentric, totally gorgeous, and completely and totally interested in dating the nerdiest kids around. I would have loved to date Danika, but she wasn't the slightest bit interested in anybody like me.

At this point, I also had become friends with Mitch. Mitch was a college dropout who had realized that he could make a living selling pot to his peers. I met Mitch when I was looking for a sustainable source of weight. Initially, we partnered up after I discovered that Harry could grow plants. Within twenty-four hours of meeting Harry, going to his apartment, and seeing the plant and the hydroponic system growing, I met with Mitch; and we agreed to fund Harry's passion project to grow plants. We found an apartment next to a church, put a deposit on it, and proceeded to purchase everything you would need for indoor gardening. We started our grow operation and never looked back.

At the time I was keeping very busy. I always had more than one iron in the fire. I had the marketing company, the grow project, I sold pot, and I had the job that Michael offered me. Here's the thing about working for Michael. I went in for a few weeks and then stopped going but continued to be paid because the company was getting more than enough work done. It was a no-show job. I made sure to see Michael every few weeks to show him my appreciation, talk about everything legal I was doing, see what was going on in his life, and avoid everything questionable in mine.

I had multiple revenue streams and felt like I was at the top of my game. And then I met Robert. Robert was one of the most enthralling men I ever met. He was another free spirit who hustled his way through life. He had partied his way out of college, but he supported himself by working for his parents' multiple businesses and supplementing his income by dealing. He was as handsome as Nathan and caught the eye of almost every girl he came across. I met him on a night of partying with my roommates (Richard S. and roommate). He was sitting in my apartment next to me fooling around with a girl on his lap and having a conversation with me like nothing was going on. After I met him, he slowly became a fixture in my apartment.

At some point in time around then, Mitch came into a lot of magic mushrooms. There was a lot going on. I had outgrown Bob's supply chain by far at this point. He had started growing plants in his apartment. In a fit of paranoia and because of the advice of a really shitty neighbor, he decided the cops must know where he was and what he was doing. Bob decided to move over a hundred plants out of his loft and somewhere that nobody knew about. Bob rented a storage unit on the other side of Rhode Island, I rented a truck, and we moved all the plants one afternoon by covering them in trash bags and moving them as quickly as we could manage. That's what you do for people who unquestionably helped you: you put yourself on the line for them.

Here's the catch. I took one container from Bob's apartment that had at some point in time contained pot and put it in the back of my truck. Now for to be chronologically correct, this is actually still back when I was living with Richard. I drove home from Bob's apartment after moving all the plants, and something curious happened: a cop pulled me over. I knew I had nothing incriminating in the vehicle, but I was still puzzled as to why I was being pulled over. The cop came up to my window and asked me if this vehicle was registered to me. I said yes, and he asked me to get out of the truck because according to him the vehicle was not registered. I asked him to check the registration and the VIN, but he refused and repeated the command to get out of the vehicle.

I went to the side of the road, and he proceeded to search the vehicle. At the time, I had all types of painting supplies and tools boxed in the front seat, which he pulled out and examined. Then he checked the bed; and as he walked up to the trash bag that held the container that had pot in it, I knew he wouldn't just let me go. A feeling of dread descended as he took out the container, opened it, and sniffed it. We both knew what the smell was.

The cop called in additional support, a drug-sniffing dog, and two detectives. I waited as they slowly arrived with an air of nervousness. The dog proceeded to go through my truck biting and sniffing everything while the two detectives began a classic good-cop, bad-cop routine on me.

As one detective was pleasant and asked what I was doing, the other one started to grill me and ask where the drugs were, who I got them from, and what I was doing with this suspicious container. I was nervous and anxious and a little rattled by their conversations, so I said it was just trash from work. I started watching the dog biting at a box of caulk, and I laughed out loud and said to the detectives, "Your dog really likes my caulk ." (Which sounds like cock.) The response was swift and immediate. The bad cop got right in my face. I looked him in the eyes, and he said. "You better watch my lips when I am talking to you. Don't you know how serious this is?" and I responded "I'd rather look you in the eyes." The questions stopped when the dog didn't find anything, and I had to eventually walk home. I lost five pounds that day.

But why was I pulled over? In the aftermath, I remembered months previous, I was driving home from rock climbing with Nathan's future wife and being pulled over. The cop told me there was an error in my registration and to go to the DMV, which I forgot about.

After the cops let me go and impounded my vehicle, I went to the DMV; and they helped me faster and better than any service I had ever gotten anywhere. They gave me proof that it was a DMV error, and I went to court. When I was in court, I got the sense the judge knew the circumstances of my impounded vehicle because when it was my turn on the docket he simply said something along the lines of "What do you have to say for yourself?" I handed over the proof that the DMV made the mistake, and my case was dismissed. The court gave me back my vehicle; and after a week, I even got a check in the mail to reimburse me for the impound fees.

This may have been the beginning of doubts forming in my mind about what I was doing. Up until then, I had no run-ins with the law. Rhode Island seemed to be very liberal and not very concerned with the presence of so much pot. You may be asking yourself why I took so many risks and potentially skirted so many laws. I know if I had been convicted of all the things that I did, I could have gone away for a long time. However, I felt as if I could manage this roller-coaster ride of drugs, money, networking, adventure, and awakenings. I wanted to do everything at once.

As for the voices, I got two warnings about what I was doing before starting down yet another path of drug exploration. This is actually backing up a bit to before Richard moved out. One night, while I was in my room, I was writing down my thoughts; and I stopped thinking. As if by magic, I wrote down, "The bigger you get, the more you will destroy." To this day, I have kept this thought in the back of my mind. However, it currently is losing its salience. The other event worth noting was that when I was in my room after a night of partying, I heard a voice say, "Leave here and never come back." I think it may have been trying to protect me from what was happening; but in truth, I resisted when the voices told me things, so what would be the point of saying that unless the purpose was to make me stick to my guns and engage even further into exploration and experimentation?

Despite the warnings, I had become enthralled by the people that were passing through my life. Networking was easy. Everybody had friends that smoked. The people that I mentioned in this chapter hold a nostalgic place in my heart. If things had gone differently I would still be talking to them instead of wondering what happened to them. These people were my druggie friends.

The thing that I learned about drug culture is that there is always somebody holding and that person becomes sought after. Some of the people I mentioned were genuinely friends with me, but the drugs and money slowly but surely began to define my friendships. I was always holding and I gained a reputation for being honest, easy, and flush with product.

Initially I made friends with my downstairs neighbors Nathan and Joseph as an ambition painter, but my relationship with them and others would end as Chance the dealer that just could not stop himself.

9 LSD

And so, then I had my first foray into the delightful world of LSD. Now with mushrooms and LSD, the key to taking them is to have the proper environmental set and setting. This isn't according to me. This is according to the researchers who became experts in the field of psychedelic research in the fifties, sixties, and seventies. Of course my first experience was a bit more fantastic and extravagant because I was not following any protocols for taking LSD. I was experimenting socially and doing as many unknowing youth had done before me; tripping out in the chaotic world.

For some reason, my friends and I heard about a Pink Floyd laser light show; and I decided that we all should go and get tickets and see it. I don't remember who brought the LSD or who had the idea to use it; but Mitch, two other friends, and I who fit prominently into my story got together and took the acid before going to the show. A lot happened on my first LSD trip.

As we went to the show, we were all in great spirits. We were exuberant and excited to the point that we were all singing along to the radio at the top of our lungs. When we got to the theater in downtown Providence, we had to wait outside; and the LSD slowly started creeping into my awareness.

I saw buildings in the distance breathe and look like they were cartoons. Harry was meeting us there, so we told the woman at the ticket counter to hold a ticket for the guy who looked like a monkey. (She recognized him immediately and let him right in and laughed the whole way.) So we made our way into the theater. The carpets were repetitively patterned and mesmerizing; and before the show, we bought these optical-illusion glasses that split your field of vision like a kaleidoscope.

We filed in and found seats while people were slowly making their way down the aisles. AC/DC came on the speakers really loud with "Highway to Hell." My immediate reaction was *Oh shit, we are not supposed to be here*, and

I started getting anxious. I eventually realized everything was OK and relaxed into the experience. However I was highly suggestable. We put on our glasses, and I experienced the most sensory input I ever have had. We were listening to "Dark Side of the Moon" by Pink Floyd with a laser show and neon lights and it was all magnified through the kaleidoscope glasses. To this day, it is one of my top experiences of my lifetime.

During this onslaught of sensory input, a few strange things happened. For one thing, Mitch started acting like a girl and was rubbing legs with me. For the rest of the night, I regarded him as being feminine and treated him almost like I would treat a date. He was flirty and really feminine. That's the best way to describe him. At around the same time as I was sitting uncomfortably trying to navigate my relationship with Mitch, I felt a point moving through my neck and physically lifting me up so as to take me out of my seat. It was very uncomfortable and felt like some otherworldly force was trying to either pull something out of me or make me move.

When the force became too much, I said to myself, *Absorb it*, referring to whatever was being pulled on; and immediately the whole force stopped. But I was still fighting something about the experience. I was so enthralled and absorbed in the light show that I didn't realize I was grinding my shin into the seat in front of me to stay grounded. Otherwise, I don't know what kind of experience I may have had. I ended up with bruises all up and down my shin.

After the performance was over, I felt as if a light switch had flipped. The relief from the absence of sensory information was palpable, and I really had nothing to say. I really found it difficult to communicate for the rest of the night. When I got back from the light show, I managed to scare the daylights out of Joseph. We went back to my apartment and were all hanging out in the living room, my friends were talking, and I was looking at my apartment floors.

The apartment had been a needle factory back in the day, and there were still needles in between the wide pine floorboards. And the boards were all beaten up and rough and partially finished. It was truly a beautiful example of age and ware, and I was admiring how sturdy the building I lived in was despite the lack of level floors or even the hole in the floor in the hallway.

In that moment, I wanted to get across how sturdy the apartment was; so I pulled the rug up and proceeded to jump up and down as high as I could in the air and slam into the floor. The noise and action took everybody by surprise especially Joseph who was downstairs studying. All of a sudden, he heard this terrible banging from above. I pointed to the floor and tried to explain what I had observed about how great my apartment's character was to my friends in the room, and Joseph came upstairs to see what was going on. All my friends were mixing, and everything just felt right.

That night we stayed up late into the night and walked around by the bay and didn't really talk, but we were together. I feel bad that I eventually had a falling out with these people; but I eventually got to a point where I couldn't handle any more of it; the stress, the paranoia, the responsibility, the greed, the maintenance, and the looming possibility that it could all go up in smoke if any of my best friends were caught breaking the law. It seemed impossibly unfair that we could be considered deviants for braving prohibition and hustling our way through life.

That night and the LSD experience was a turning point for me. I felt as though I was high on life and it was okay to do crazy things. It was becoming normal to take psychedelics, to hear voices, to probe the limits of human experience. I had had mixed experiences with psychedelics but I was becoming intrigued by the expansion of what was possible to experience. It was like a whole new world was opening up to me. I was not some cautious, prepped, and educated explorer. I was experiencing the adventure and consequences of living off the cuff and taking chances. In a way I was gambling and I did not have the discipline to hold back for long

10 VENTURES AND MISADVENTURES

As I started to legitimately work with more and more people, I started to consider a way out of all the illegal endeavors I had undergone. I had bound myself to the fates of so many people, and they had come to rely on me to come up with new ideas and networking so that we could all progress, or so I thought. I didn't just make the realization that they could get by without me. I felt as though I had made my own place, and I wanted to keep it; but at the same time, I knew it wasn't a sustainable trajectory because at heart I knew that what I really was trying to do was express my need for interconnectedness. I hadn't yet viewed my journey as that of a quest for love or spirituality. My goals were not right for my heart, and my activities were growing more and more risky at every turn.

When Richard S. and his roommate moved in. As I was saying before, Mitch came into a large quantity of magic mushrooms. I took some off his hand and proceeded to distribute them liberally to close friends. That was where Robert and Marissa came in. I started to drink mushroom tea with Robert and Marissa on the regular. At this point, I had stopped doing the marketing company; and the project with Daniel was nearing its first stage of completion.

Daniel and I had talked to friends and made plans to have his schoolmates move in, in a few months because Richard S. and his roommate had expressed their need to move on. I had invested about $25,000 in Socialite to date, and we had hired a software firm to develop the front end of the app while Daniel tirelessly toiled on the back end, which he never tried to explain to me. I was under the impression that all I would have to invest was $25,000, and we would have a finished product; but the farther we got, the more it seemed that we would have to get more money.

We tried to join a tech incubator in Boston to fund the company, get experienced mentors, and get a support staff and a free office. Daniel did an amazing job articulating what the project's goal was, but they didn't bite. Unfortunately, I think they realized that we were working on a soon-to-be redundant product. If Facebook came out with a mobile product, it would essentially render us irrelevant. And as we got closer and closer to the end of the work that could be done with the money that I had invested, I started to do more mephedrone and more mushrooms.

At some point around then, after experiencing so many states of altered consciousness and experiencing so many messages deterring me from staying in Rhode Island, and in combination with the paranoia that I would get caught, I started to crack under pressure. It started after a particular mushroom trip where I had the overwhelming sensation of being plugged into the world through invisible connections that seemed to come out of the world. I was lying down and just felt like connection after connection was being made to my torso, and I was so overwhelmed that I just let it happen and laid down helplessly.

After this or maybe one of the many other trips (I don't recall exactly when), I started to listen to conversations that people were having to hear what I can only describe as hidden messages. For example, I would listen to all the conversations in a restaurant and pick out words from different people and make sentences that were gibberish. This idea meshed with the idea of the collective conscious. I just thought that maybe I could start to hear what the collective was saying by paying attention to conversations around me.

Then I started really listening and observing my friends around me; and as I continued to crack up and persisted tripping, I started to have less pleasant experiences. There wasn't any specific bad trip with mushrooms, but there was with LSD and a substance called something like 2C-E. It is considered the "cocaine of psychedelics."

I wasn't the only one cracking up. Marissa had started to do a lot of mephedrone and had lost a lot of weight. Mephedrone was originally introduced in Israel as a weight loss drug because it makes you burn calories at a ridiculous rate. Unfortunately, it is also fairly habit forming, and it feels excellent because it creates dopamine dumps that last for hours. I remember seeing Marissa after we had stopped hanging out for a while, and she was so disorganized. Her eyes looked like she wasn't under control. And I can't help but think at some point I must have looked like that too. Holding it together with threads and just moving forward by sheer force. The last I heard from Marissa after we stopped talking was she had gotten pregnant and moved away. It's amazing to think that she is a mother of a seven- or eight-year-old by now. I never saw it coming.

That's the best thing and the worst thing about the world: you can plan and plan until you have your whole life planned out ahead of you and then drop dead the next day. It makes sense to plan for the worst-case scenario or prepare financially for a long life, but it's important to remember to experience moment to moment. I may have a disorganized memory of adventure and rule breaking, but I experienced so much of the time moment to moment; and since then, I have learned to really be in the moment so that it feels like my experiences were part of a past lifetime. Time may be fleeting, but if you find yourself engaged in some grand scheme that is always interesting and consuming, you can actually experience what's happening instead of zoning out and just going through the motions. Then life can really be fulfilling.

I think that that is what attracted me to Buddhism. I wasn't interested in the concept that your life was best spent living simply. I was interested in the idea of mindfulness and the path to nirvana. I only gleaned small amounts of information about Buddhism, but everything has come in handy in life, especially the idea that you should become friends with your disease. I literally am friends with the symptoms that define my disorder according to the medical model.

I don't know if anybody has done anything similar to my escapades with sanity and recovery because I haven't heard of any cases. I would like to join a support group for schizophrenia or hearing voices so that I can hear other people's experiences, but there aren't currently available to me in the area. I also hope that if I become a licensed professional counselor, I will have the opportunity to work with people with schizophrenia and other disorders on the spectrum. If I can somehow help just one person in therapy with an insight I garnered while journeying, then it will all be worth it. I already try to spread the potential that I see around to friends and family; hopefully, I can also make an impact with others like me.

11 Can't Get Out

In the past I thought that wealth was important. Being my own man was integral to life. Being independent in Rhode Island involved holding up what amounted to being my very small empire of businesses and hustles but was not going to get me to where my true self could persist. I realized very quickly as I became more and more enmeshed in the drug culture and things spiraled out of control that I was potentially going down a path that would lead to potential violence, controlling malicious manipulation, negative feelings, and desires I had never dreamt or expected to experience.

As my ventures continued to roll along, and I started to get more paranoid about getting caught, and I started to feel the stress and weight that my ventures created, I went on a trip to California to solidify my ability to provide more and more products to my dealers. The idea came up because my friend Mitch told me about another dealer who had just gotten busted for mailing product from California. The police couldn't figure out what he was doing at first, but they eventually got a hint by camping out in front of his door and seeing that packages tended to come at peak times of his business. The police ended up intercepting a package somehow, and Mitch's associate was busted.

Mitch knew the person who was on the other end of the packages in California, so he contacted the guy; and we flew out for a week to tour California, interviewed gardeners, and make purchases. This was a stressful trip and made me see that Mitch and I were friends, but we did not have a completely common vested interest unbeknownst to me.

We flew on the airplane with the most cash that we could legally take, got to California, and went to visit Todd. We met Todd's roommates and hung out for a while after picking up a big package of money we had sent, and then we set off for Northern California. It was beautiful in California because it had just rained and the countryside outside the cities was an undulating landscape of hills covered in hues of green and lush happy plants.

We drove up the highway and didn't see a single cop car on the way, so we felt safe. We were still stressed out about meeting these potential strangers because we didn't really know if we could trust them, but we took a leap of faith. We met at a hotel in a very rural part of a county near Mendocino and called a few people Mitch had connections with and waited. While we waited, we noticed a hippie-looking older man outside the hotel. I don't know how, but we ended up talking to him.

I don't recall his name, but he was a very trusting and loving man. He told us he was a grower and that somebody had recently robbed him by taking his latest crop. He talked about his family and was completely disarming for us. He showed us his product, which didn't possess the quality that we wanted. He didn't directly try to sell us anything, but I think he was hoping for interest. He was so friendly that before he left he hugged us both and told us he loved us.

In retrospect, I admire somebody with that much compassion and trust in his life. Sure, he could have been a little more cautious; but it goes to show why I like hippie culture so much. Free love—it doesn't cost a thing.

Eventually, our contact got there. He told us how he set up shop at his house and had guard dogs and was careful. We talked a little about using the mail, and he seemed open-minded. He took our money and drove away, leaving his friend behind as collateral. What did he think we'd do? Eventually, after a lot of pacing and stressing about money, which I would eventually learn to despise (the stress associated with money—what did money ever do wrong? ha-ha), our connect came back with a cornucopia of product. We tried some and made a selection, but we still had more to spend, so our connection went back out to another farm. Eventually, we spent all our money; and now we had to get our product back to Rhode Island.

That was actually the easy part. We bought a vacuum sealer and bags and some boxes and simply packaged our product and sent it to Rhode Island. Easy-peasy.

We stayed the night in the hotel, and that night Mitch got the idea to call the connect who had dealt with the dealer that had gotten popped by the cops. Mitch called and then set up a time to go see this mysterious connect in Lake Tahoe. We drove across a beautiful mountainous country the next day and drove up and up and up until the pine trees grew tall and we saw snow. It was an amazing contrast to the sunny, warm northern county.

We met this guy who basically told us that the FBI was monitoring him, that he had the PO box that he used compromised by the cops, that he had lost a lot of money in the same PO box, and that he was taking steps to disappear. He made a few demands before we could go and meet his source. He wanted a thousand dollars a week for his girlfriend in exchange for access to his main connect. We basically said let's see what deal was on the table before we agreed to anything.

He drove us across town to an establishment of some sort. I will be vague because otherwise you could probably find this establishment, and I don't want to incriminate anybody. So we arrived outside this nondescript building, rang a bell, and got buzzed in through some thick security doors. We walked down a very sketchy-looking hallway and ended up in a room with a counter that had all types of product behind it in jars. There were a few people behind the counter, and there was a very cute puppy that I think was going to be a future guard dog. The owner of the establishment came out and greeted us, and we started talking business.

We started to explain our needs, and that was when it happened. The owner told us he only wanted to deal with one person; Mitch volunteered. At the time, I didn't think anything of it. We agreed on money, method, and some further details—and that was that. Mitch got connected. This only occurred to me after we got back to Rhode Island, and he proceeded to tell me he couldn't get me any product.

I had to find my own connection to keep everything running and the cash flowing. Despite the many streams of income, I had, I was careful about what I spent and I paid my bills with legitimate means because I did not want to be accused of money laundering at the time. I still had over $10,000 of credit card bills, and money was stressing me out. I started asking around about other sources from California, and Daniel introduced me to another college student who I will call Drew. After I met Drew, I convinced him to start sending me packages; and I was in business again.

I still had a relationship with Mitch because we were funding the indoor gardening venture together, but I was really discouraged about what he did. I also had spent over $20,000 on the gardening venture with little return. That was when I met Paco.

Paco was somewhat of a pathological liar. When I saw him, he was almost always medicated with something; and he talked a big game and slurred his speech all the time. But he was friendly and had experience in gardening, so I brought him in to the operation because he just wanted to grow plants. He didn't care about getting paid as long as I kept him as a customer. It wasn't until I went to his house that I realized what a complete mess he was.

Paco lived in what amounted to a disorganized pile of garbage. It was like anything he used he just dropped in his apartment, and he never cleaned. I never saw his bedroom; but somehow, he managed to appear to have clean clothes. At one point, he was seeing two women at once and was trolling the Internet for dates on Craigslist. He was functional, just not healthy. Harry had been doing our growing up until that point but Paco didn't really get along that well; but for the moment, it shook things up.

Meanwhile, I was hanging out with Robert and using mushrooms regularly. He had become a customer and somebody to hang out with and have fun. I remember from one particularly interesting trip, he got a jar of peanut butter and told me to try a spoonful. When I tasted the peanut butter, it tasted like it was alive and was pure energy. I had never experienced any flavor like it before. It was one of those moments where I thought Robert was allowing me to experience something beyond conventional reality. I think it was during the same trip I found some face paint and went into the bathroom and painted half my face black and the other half white. Robert painted symbols on his face. We messed with everybody we saw that night, and then Danika came in with a camcorder and recorded some of the antics. I would regret that.

I started to meet Robert's friends, and he introduced me to Andrew. Now Andrew was a very talented sculptor. He was currently looking for investors, and he had a molding product that had very cool properties and allowed him to sculpt very fine detailed miniature sculptures. He specialized in faces and bodies and actually had his work published. He had all kinds of other ideas for businesses, and I was really impressed with him, so I kept on meeting him and decided I would seed his company.

It was over $20,000, but I pulled it together and got involved in yet another project. I told Mitch about the project, and he was interested in investing too; but when Andrew asked Mitch how he made his money, Mitch had no explanation, so that fell through. Andrew was the last legitimate monetary investment I would make. I, however, did get Alex to make a $10,000 investment. But even he had stopped legitimately working legitimately at that point and solely depended on me and herb to make money.

Slowly my venture with Daniel came to a halt. He started telling me that we needed more money or we wouldn't be able to continue, and I had heard that Facebook was coming out with a mobile app. I didn't pony up what we needed, and so he changed directions and started working on his own project. But just before this happened, I remember going down to Daniel's apartment a few weeks after Danika had made the video of Robert and my hallucinogenic antics.

Danika had used the footage in one of her classes to show what she could do with special effects. At the time, I didn't know if I was high or what; but I remember watching a video of me in my black-and-white face talking to Robert with the symbols on his face. No sound was coming out of our mouths, and the colors on my face were enhanced when Robert talked. All kinds of animated pot leaves and drugs came out of his mouth. Then it cut to a picture of a floating futuristic city with a psychedelic background, and then the words "Stop trying to contact us" and "Your city is burning" came up in big letters.

At that point, very small symbols were having a great effect on what I was thinking; and when I saw the video, I was horrified and thought the world I was creating was essentially burning. I was in total distress. Around that time, my health was catching up with me. The constant stress was making me experience a fibromyalgia-like set of symptoms where I was always in pain. I was burning out, and I was having trouble walking. I was starting to feel like an old man. That didn't stop me from taking mushrooms, and I would take them with random people I had never met if Robert was there.

I remember taking them in this cute girl's apartment in Providence. I don't remember their names, but there was a skinny girl and a chubby girl. I liked the skinny girl; the skinny girl was attracted to Robert, and the chubby girl was attracted to me. At the time, Robert was in a serious relationship. He knew how to flirt and remain completely faithful. I knew I needed to do something about my health when I had trouble sitting down and standing up regularly. I started getting massages every day from Marissa and stretching in the heat on my roof. That helped, but I was still suffering.

That's when I started buying LSD in large quantities. I don't remember where I got it from, but I would get pieces of colorful paper that I had to cut into little squares. I stopped doing mushrooms because they had run out, and I was not doing mephedrone regularly despite some fun experiences. I saw that it was really habit forming, and I didn't want to get addicted.

Right around then, Richard S. and his roommate decided to move out. Apparently, Richard S. was trying to get clean from an opioid habit to no avail; and he was moving home to help himself. He either graduated or was trying to put himself in a puritanical situation; either way, I don't have a clear recollection of what occurred. I just recall a few instances of Richard S's fragile attempts to get clean that ending up in a series of withdrawals that ended in a lot of hallucinations that should have gotten him admitted.

I didn't want to have to pay for the whole rent myself; and by chance, a student who went to school near me and knew Paco heard about me and ended up at my apartment. Her name was Andrea; and as soon as I met her, I thought she was something special. She had long blonde hair and was naturally beautiful, confident, and interesting. I know that she had dealt in the past. I think she put herself through culinary school. She had been on the drug scene for a while, but I really don't recall her ever doing any drugs with me around. She did get me to try methamphetamine, which I didn't really enjoy. When she came over, she happened to tell me that she was on the apartment search, and I told her I was looking for roommates, so she could move in if she agreed to the rent.

Daniel was pissed because I had agreed for his friends to move in, but I would have to live alone for two months, and I was trying to spend as little money as possible, so I opted for new roommates.

My other new roommate was Tyler. He was a very confident young hustler who worked at a strip club and got by doing what he had to. I don't know that I liked him immediately, but he had been living with Andrea, so I didn't think he could be that bad. They also would eventually bring two more roomies to the apartment who I didn't really talk to or interact with that much, and I don't remember their names for the life of me.

After Andrea and Tyler moved in, I started doing LSD recreationally. That's when I started having bad trips. The first time I tripped alone, I remember a few things happened. First of all, I was alone in the apartment. When I started to come up, I was sitting on a chair, and I lay back and started to feel like I was choking. I couldn't breathe; and when I closed my eyes, I saw glowing naked neon idols in the shape of women looking at me, and then I heard mocking laughter, and I suddenly felt very ashamed. I also had the experience where I really had to urinate all of a sudden, so I ran over to the bathroom and emptied my bladder, and then it happened again like ten minutes later. I don't know where all the fluids even came from. It seemed like something was playing with me like a kid plays with the TV remote or the light switch.

During another trip when Andrea and her friends were downstairs with me, I found myself in the mirror in the bathroom, and I heard somebody tell me to "Come out" like they were talking to me telepathically. I really freaked out and went upstairs. I hid in my room for the rest of the night doubting what I heard and being afraid of the potential mind-bending experience that another person could access my mind.

A few other events happened that stand out in my mind when I had bad trips. One night, I couldn't sleep. I lay in my room. I heard all these really loud explosions; and when I looked out my window, I saw two cop cars across the street, which freaked me out even more because I was already regularly paranoid about possessing so many substances. In my mind a story was playing out that unseen supernatural forces were breaking me out of a prison of sorts. Forces were battling for control of me and the explosions were the attacks of new beings that were trying to break me free. I had a lot of thoughts like this that would last for months.

Another time I was tripping was when Andrea was around. I was sitting in the room with a bunch of her friends, just listening and thinking a stream of consciousness to myself. All of a sudden, I sensed the presence of a massive, huge being coming crashing down on me. Then Andrea was telling me to stop thinking. That really freaked me out because it seemed as if she was in on what I was experiencing. After that, when Andrea and her friends were over, I started to sit very still and started to stop breathing, which partially led to the idea being implanted in my mind that I should stop breathing.

Andrea went traveling for the summer, and I was left with Tyler and the other roommates. I was still working with Andrew and dealing with Alex, but now I had time on my hands after the mobile app project ended. I just kind of hung around with people and started having obsessive thoughts. I started to attribute events happening to other people's intervention. I started to think that when people were talking about one another, they were really referring to me. My world really started to spiral, but the LSD made me feel less and less pain from the fibromyalgia, so I continued using it.

Just before Andrea left for the summer, Tyler brought home a few pills of the "psychedelic cocaine" that I mentioned earlier. I took it with Robert, and I remember a few different moments from that trip. The first thing that happened as I came up was that I felt my lungs vibrate and oscillate uncontrollably like there were flashing LED lights and strobe lights all going off at once inside, and I had the feeling of undulation energy going back and forth between my lungs. It was an amazing energy that felt electric and energizing all at once. I don't think there are really words to describe the experience.

At some point, Robert went off into the night, and I was left alone and started freaking out, so I called Rick. He came over like a good friend would and then told me, "Let them experiment on you." Then I got the sensation that my head was cut off and put in a glass jar, and I heard the bubbles all around me. I even heard a chain saw running and felt as it cut into my neck and heard corresponding resistance. It was terrifying but I didn't see any of this happening. My mind definitely believed on some level it happened.

Rick eventually went home, but this chemical lasted for twenty-four hours. I spent the early hours of the morning on the couch lying face down in a blanket convinced that I shouldn't breathe. I was generally panicking and struggling to hold my breath for hours. At some point, Tyler came and tried to console me; and he rubbed my back, which made me feel so much better. But I just lay on the couch awake for hours while my apartment mates went on with their lives quietly and didn't really seem concerned with me at all.

This really sucked because I was just hoping somebody would sit with me and stay with me while I came back from the chemical. I really wish Robert hadn't left, but I know he wanted to go have an adventure. Apparently, he had a great time exploring while I suffered alone in my apartment where I no longer felt comfortable or wanted.

I should mention that the time of my bad trips I was being introduced to new people all of the time and I was really not comfortable with anybody. All my roommates thought I was a business genius because of the money I was making, the investments, and the way I was dealing. In some ways my position was a barrier between myself and others. It was like they put me on a pedestal and were afraid to really engage with me. The drugs, the paranoia, the secrecy, and the people around me began to really make me feel isolated. I didn't have anybody that actually knew what was going on with me. Keeping everything to myself was starting to make my unstable experiences fester as I couldn't figure out how to make meaning of what was happening to me.

12 VIOLENT AND DISGUSTING THOUGHTS

Now we get to the part of my history where my overall trajectory changed, when I metaphorically had a gun to the head of the one I was scuffling with. Or at least the seeds that led me to that metaphor.

Before Richard S. and his roommate moved out, they had allowed a young girl to move in. She was about twenty-one. She was beautiful but was an utter mess. She wasn't going to school, she had no job, and she had been kicked out of the house. She was part of the group that used mephedrone habitually.

She lived in our house in the room that was a closet upstairs without ventilation, and she lived off charity and stuck around the house. At the time, a few things were culminating. I had a huge argument with Richard S. because his addiction was putting me at risk as a dealer, and I was so pissed at him that I had yelled, "Don't you realize I am a drug lord!" It was a little over the top, but I was trying to see the danger he was putting me in. I felt like one of my friends was going to slip up and I was going to lose everything. I had the same general feeling about this charity-case girl.

I had talked to my connections and had gotten her a job. She was a pretty girl, and I must say that I had thought that it would be interesting to get with her; but at the time my roommate that I cannot recall the name of, who had a girlfriend, was essentially trying to sleep with this runaway. There were complications if I did anything with her.

One night, we were all on mephedrone in our underwear on the couch in the living room, and I was feeling particularly good having pleasure cascade down my body. All the while, I was completely engaged in nothing but the sheer feeling I was experiencing and simultaneously having the confidence to talk to a sober girl who was fully dressed and Marissa. At this point, I had it in my head that Marissa had a thing for me, but I was lusting after another friend who was sitting next to her.

When Marissa left the room, I told the other girl directly that I was thinking about what I really wanted the other night and that an image of her body floated through my mind after I prompted myself. A little while later, the runaway girl came up behind everybody, looked at me and tried to get naked in the middle of the room. She was under the influence of mephedrone so this was not really unusual. I don't know what her intentions were, but the other roommate that I cannot recall the name of was like "Whoa, hold on there" and put a shirt on her.

Despite talking to the other girl I was interested in, the runaway had piqued my interest. Mephedrone had an effect on you where you just felt good and confident about doing everything and comfortable about being with people. Somehow that night five or six of us ended up all in the runaway girl's bed in the tiny closet upstairs, innocently hanging out in underwear and lingerie, lying back in the air, kicking our legs up, and laughing. It was beautiful. There was one point where things got awkward. We could have had an orgy if somebody had started getting sexual, but it wasn't really what the mood was. We were feeling giddy and free, but runaway girl got upset and broke up the event by getting up and leaving.

In retrospect, I feel as if these people were becoming a part of my family; they had already become one another's family and support, and it would be kind of incestuous to have sex with everybody. I think they began to realize that and started to desire normal relationships.

But runaway girl was having trouble keeping a job and interacting with a lot of men who wanted her for sex, but I know she was thankful to me and tried to express it by expressing to me interest in finding me clients to deal to. I appreciated the idea, but I still kind of considered her a fuck-up on some level when I was not on mephedrone.

Now my feelings about the runaway girl also related to my feeling for Mitch. Around this time, I had invested time and money into the plant growing operation with Mitch while I tried to help him to find a legitimate form of income. We still hung out, but I was uncomfortable with his friends and still had some lingering confusion thanks to our epic psychedelic trip together when he was acting like a girl toward me. At this point, Mitch had started seeing a gorgeous girl from college, and I was becoming jealous of the ease at which he appeared to be surpassing my success because of his good luck in life and the very reliable connection that he had gotten in California.

At some point, I was over at Mitch's house; and he told me something that made me turn white as a sheet and feel totally and utterly betrayed by him. I don't remember what he said. I just remember the emotional state I was in and the sinking feeling in my stomach. It made me start looking at him in a new light as if he was an obstacle, a competition, and an adversary.

We still had the indoor gardening project together; and after investing so much money, we finally had our first successful grow cycle. I went over to the house, harvested our crop, processed it, and sold it without saying a thing to Mitch about it. I figured I would screw him over.

At the same time, I started having homicidal thoughts. I thought I could take over Mitch's business for some reason. It was a sign of my greed for power. I started to think of ways to murder Mitch. I considered getting a gun, inviting him for a stroll along the river walk after midnight, and executing him if nobody was around. I was in the very early plans of this and was not convinced it was a good idea, but I know that's how any premediated act happens. It's a synthesis of thought, aggravation, and breaking point.

Luckily, I prevented reaching that breaking point while tripping. I don't know what other significant events occurred during this LSD trip. I just know I was in my room and I was having terrible thoughts about what could happen to me if the runaway girl fucked up. For some reason, I thought she could somehow bring me down. The fact that Mitch was screwing me over and was so happy and successful really was making me jealous. And all of a sudden, I thought about strangling the runaway girl to death.

I had a feeling come over me like the essence of sinister power surge through my being. It was the most disturbing comprehension of what it feels like to take away one's life. It was not necessarily a "bad" sensation. But I never felt it before, and I never want to feel it again. It was like the embodiment of the sensation of manipulative control. Even now, recalling the feeling makes me feel sick in the pit of my stomach.

That was the night that convinced me that I had to get out of the business I was in before I did something stupid, that I would regret, and that would forever change my trajectory to a life of what I could consider focused on selfishness, evil, manipulation, and greed. The problem was that I couldn't find a way to give up the money without causing myself to totally and utterly break down, give up, and crush my ambitions and all I had worked so hard for.

13 BACKING UP A BIT

Now a few months before this, I met one other person of note, who I have had contact with on and off again because he always seemed like a standup guy. He was interesting, charismatic, connected, very careful, and discreet. He helped me on a spiritual level when I was at my worst with actions that he appeared to have committed metaphysically but showed no physical sign of committing. He also has been sincerely interested in my life since we met. He was the only person who would reach out to me to find out how I was doing throughout the years since we met, even though we only hung out a few times. The more I learn about him, the more I like him; and I believe him to be a truly constructive, positive human being. I will call him Theo for now.

I met Theo through Paco. Theo had been dealing high-end product in a city in Pennsylvania since he had gone to jail. He hasn't told me too much of the why of going to jail, but he has alluded to the lingering effects of feelings of isolation and loneliness associated with being jailed for a long period. I will not say much more about his current life other than it appears he has gone completely legit. I just know he hasn't alluded to marijuana much since the last few times we had an exchange unless we were talking about history.

Paco invited Theo to Rhode Island because Theo had a company that was related to gardening. Paco had convinced Theo to come visit somehow; and when Theo came, Paco first brought him to meet me. At the time, Theo was looking for a reliable source of product, and I was the closest thing Paco had encountered. But here's the thing. Theo was supposed to stay the night over Paco's house, which looked like a bombshell had gone off and where there was no clean surface, but Theo did not yet know this.

First, Theo met me, and we talked very candidly about business, and he expressed interest in getting some weight. I thought he could become a potential new customer, so I gave him what I had at a steal and basically lost out on a lot of money. Then we went over to Paco's house, and Theo proceeded to pull me aside.

Theo liked cleanliness and order and was disgusted by Paco's house. Theo pulled me aside. "What should I do here?" I saw his distress and offered him my couch and apartment. At the time, there were not going to be any roommates around, and so he stayed over.

That night, we talked about the businesses we ran and the product we sold and even the plants we were growing and had grown and his connections to California. I told him about my trip to California and the packages I was getting and essentially sold him on Mitch and my model of doing business. He also met Mitch who he admitted he was not as impressed with. This is at a time when I hadn't started doing LSD yet, so I was altogether very polished.

That launched our friendship. We would keep in touch. I would eventually agree to bring him a whole mess of baby plants and visit him in Pennsylvania and help him set up shop indoor gardening, which he had more experience with than I did.

We would talk on our burner phones every now and again about business and ideas and how he had progressed with packages. Apparently, he knew a network of growers back in California and had been to conventions and networked extensively.

Knowing Theo has historically been a constant temptation for me. Since I eventually stopped dealing and moved home to Connecticut, I have talked to Theo every few years and recalled him telling me that one day maybe we could go into business together. As of the last time I talked to him, I am relieved that he only reminisces with me and has no longer mentioned that he is doing anything but managing a construction business.

As we have communicated throughout the last seven years, every time we talked, I would always struggle with the desire to start up dealing again. I knew I could save some money, make a deal with Theo, and start all over from scratch. The thought has occurred to me several times, especially with all the talk in Connecticut about legalizing recreational marijuana.

I feel as if this is a test. So far, I have not relapsed into anything but have a string of thoughts about how I could make easy money and move out of my parents' house and get my feet under myself again.

14 BIRTHDAY BLUES

It was my twenty-seventh birthday. This was my most humiliating birthday to date. It should have been entertaining and happy, but I ended up spending it at a strip club. There was no woman I was friends with there, which sucked. I was with all the guys who worked for me and dealt with me. I was in the VIP section because my friends decided to show they "cared" by spending a lot of money and getting bottle service.

This actually occurred before Daniel had moved out and before Tyler and Andrea moved in, but it struck me as some additional fodder for starting to really have a sense that I was not among people who were really standup guys. Alex knew a lot of the strippers because he frequented that scene. He picked out two strippers and told me I was getting a surprise. I usually think surprises are good. I was skeptical, but I agreed to participate in whatever he was planning.

These two beautiful women escorted me to the bathroom where a guy was waiting with a pair of boxers. I was trying to talk to the strippers to find out what was going to happen, but they were tight-lipped. I was told to go into the bathroom and take off all my clothes but the boxers. At that point, I nearly abandoned ship; but I figured everybody had spent a lot of money on whatever this was, so I just went with it.

I came out of the bathroom in my boxers, and a spotlight shone on me. The two women escorted me to a booth on the stage in front of about fifty random men. I am really sure that they were high-class citizens at this point.

I ended up getting a striptease from two women in the booth, which I really did not enjoy. The booth was also a shower, so I was getting hit with hot water. I guess this could have been enjoyable for some men, but at the time I was a very private person who kept out of the spotlight. Then the DJ started saying, "This is Chance, founder of Little Software!" And my heart sank because I had no faith in my tech endeavor any longer.

I felt like I was on display for everybody and that I was living some life that was just not me. I wasn't really comfortable in strip clubs. I wasn't really a great entrepreneur unless you count pot, and it all was reflected in the way the experience made me feel completely humiliated for who I had become and how I was acting.

What made it worse was after a very short dance, the girls poured a pitcher of ice down my boxers. Let me tell you I was not even the slightest bit aroused to begin with. Then Mitch came up to the booth and shoved like $50 or more of singles through the slot into the booth. I was dumbstruck. The worst part was that they also videotaped it. I doubt anybody even knows they have that tape anymore. It just looks like some guy standing there looking totally blank with a bunch of beautiful women dancing all over him naked. He totally looks like he doesn't know what to do because he wishes he was somewhere completely different.

In retrospect, they might have meant well, but they really didn't know me well enough. This would make me doubt everything I was doing even more. The only good thing was that I guess everybody got the sense that I didn't want to really ever talk about that night again. I never heard of anybody reminiscing about it like it was a great night everybody remembered.

After Andrea and Tyler moved in, I found myself falling for Andrea. Despite the strange thoughts and behaviors I was having, I still was falling for her; but she wasn't really accessible to me. She would invite over all kinds of people. She invited over an old hippie who cooked meth, and then she would invite over friends from culinary school. It was always a surprise. I got acquainted with a particular rapscallion named Bobby who was a fellow culinary school graduate and happened to work as a personal chef of the president of a very popular football team.

Concurrently to meeting Bobby, I started spending a lot of time with Alex. He was one of my best customers, and we were trying to figure out ways to go legit. In addition to investing in Andrew, we also decided to start a company that was focused on art. The idea was to create a community of artists who were amenable to us that we could eventually help advance their careers with management or representation. We found a venue that sold custom jewelry that said they would host a party. Then I proceeded to trawl the Internet for any illustrators, graffiti artists, sculptors, or really anybody who performed. I e-mailed them and told them that they were invited to a free event to network and meet with us.

I talked to Bobby, and he agreed to cook a tasting menu of items, so we invested $300 in groceries. He cooked all day in my apartment the day of the event. We got wine and drinks and everything we thought a party needed. We set up tables in the jewelry studio and talked to the owners and waited to see what would happen. To out delight, about thirty artists came, some even with their families. It was the most positive idea I had pursued, and it was a complete success. Everybody had a great time and said they would be interested in doing it again.

I would also try to work with a successful club promoter and magazine owner in Rhode Island to bring the spotlight to the art project. Alex and I made a deal that we would provide some entertainment at a club in the form of graffiti artists and my friend Brian who had also created rap and alternative music CDs.

I went and bought a few bolts of canvas and some wood and built some huge 8x8 canvasses and some smaller ones. We met with the graffiti artists, and they seemed excited. Brian seemed cocky and brought in of his CDs. I kind of hoped this also could inspire him to start performing.

The night went well, the graffiti artists got a lot of attention, and then when Brian went on to rap, he used a track with the lyrics already on it. He didn't really seem prepared to perform. But the group he brought loved it. So overall everything went well until I went outside.

I remember walking down the sidewalk and seeing two beautiful women walking down the street with the club manager. I remember being very attracted to them and had some very lewd thoughts. As soon as I had thought it, they made some disgusted sounds, turned around, and went in the other direction of me.

During that period of time I had smoked and taken LSD in the recent past and was still experiencing bizarre side effects that night, I thought that people could hear my thoughts; and so I started talking to people around me by thinking narratives in my head. Unfortunately, it had the effect that sometimes when I wanted to say something to somebody, I would think it internally instead. Then discouraged by the lack of response but not convinced I was wrong, I would just continue trying to think conversations with others. The worst part was it seemed that my timing of having lewd or crude thoughts had an impact on people around me.

I started really getting more and more paranoid that people could hear my thoughts and were only responding when they wanted to. It made me further listen to other people's conversations for clues of what they were thinking and really wanted to say to me. I remember being in many situations where I would be hanging out with a group of people; and no matter what I tried to do, I couldn't get a word in. Whenever I tried to talk, somebody else would pipe in just before I spoke. This happened many times when I hung out in groups, and it further made me feel isolated and made me more and more of an observer.

I still took care of business and talked to Steve O, Michael, and all my dealers like nothing was wrong; but it couldn't be further from the truth.

Rick was starting to spend a lot of time in my apartment because he was smitten with Andrea as well. He would just show up all the time to be around her. He started to figure into my search for meaning of what was happening more and more.

Right before the summer Andrea went to California, I got up the courage to tell her I was attracted to her; and she told me she was leaving but to wait for her. Now Andrea did have some idea that there was something wrong with me. She actually tried to help me a few times. After a particularly bad trip, she invited me on a road trip to go to a music festival with VIP backstage access. At that point, I was scared shitless of doing anything like that, and I declined.

Then after seeing me in constant states of despair, she asked me if I wanted to have a funeral for myself in order to be reborn. I figured I would try what she thought would work. One night about a week later, my roommates and I went to a graveyard after dark. They had me lie down on a sheet, and all said a few words about what they would miss about me. Then Andrea asked me what to call myself, and I figured my middle name was John, so I told her John; and for about a week, she called me Johnny until she saw that the funeral didn't really work.

I remember her also telling me that I should go do something crazy like jump off a high rock into a river or something to get my spirits and adrenaline up. She cared enough to tell me that she had to rebuild herself at some point after tripping and that she knew what I was going through, but I still don't know after seven years of not talking to her.

Andrea was one of the many beautiful people I met on my journey who I ended contact with after I moved from Rhode Island. The more I write about these people, the more I miss the good times with them and the more I remember that I was really unwell. Even Steve O saw me and suggested that I could go see somebody and get help.

I feel anxious writing about this because I have had so many intense experiences; but at the time, I really didn't have the full picture of who I was or what was happening. I remember so many events that point to some type of spiritual awakening and spiritual experience; but at the time, I was torn between the acceptance of my childhood, adolescence, and early adulthood, believing that there was essentially nothing important in life beyond logic and the mysterious world of visions, hallucinations, intense emotional, and sensory experiences. Their lasting imprint would be psychosomatic symptoms that I began to experience without end.

On some level, some part of me just kept on repressing these experiences that I was having, and that same part of me kept trying to live on like it was business as usual without truly ever choosing to integrate my experiences into a cogent overall paradigm of living. I was living in a state of denial, and I believe that I continued to take these psychoactive substances in an attempt to break the part of me that was determined to guide me down a path of ignorance.

15 WOMEN

I left off talking about Andrea. She left for the summer, and some great things were happening at the time. It was near the end of the semester of college, and I was getting access to the promoter that I had talked with about my art rep project. Through his connections, I got invited to a few clubs; and I started going out more. One night in particular, I went to a hotel and was admitted to the VIP room with Robert and his friends from college. We were just celebrating everything, but I remembered one particular event.

There was a girl there who was a total conservative snob that I found myself totally into, and she asked what I did. At that moment, I knew exactly who I was and who I wanted to be. I was able to tell her about all the projects that I was doing and my entrepreneurship and what I was accomplishing, but at the same time I left out the dealing and couldn't be truly honest. I knew who I was, and dealing was not part of that image. The girl happened to be waiting for her boyfriend to my dismay. But her friend Amanda, who was a little chubbier than I am used to, seemed really into me.

I ended up thinking that I might as well have fun even if I don't get the girl I wanted. I danced with Amanda who was slightly awkward, drunk, and yet totally into the moment. The music wasn't great, but we had fun, and everybody went back to my place. I ended hooking up Amanda, and then we hung out the next night and hooked up and the next night and the next.

It was nice. We had no real agreement about what our relationship was or any real expectations, but my feelings for her kept growing until I finally found out her plans for graduation to join the peace corps and go on a three-year adventure.

Before our relationship ended, I took LSD one night by myself; and a bunch of friends came over. I remember sitting on the floor while everybody else sat on the couch. Rick was there, and he looked exhausted. All of a sudden, I got the sense that I should go outside. I went to the door, and I saw a path literally highlighted on the floor leading out the door. So what did I do? I went back inside and sat back down.

Rick told me that I had to make a decision, but I wasn't hearing it. Everybody else who was sitting around seemed to have nothing to say and didn't look very happy with me. In my mind, I was thinking that there were only two choices: stay or go. I could follow the path set before me, or I could avoid it. Then I thought to myself I want a third option. At that moment, I didn't know it; but I was starting on a journey that would redefine life as I knew it. It would change my behaviors, my stability, my understanding of the world and how I related to it and would crystalize a new way of being for me.

After Amanda went off into the world, I was romantically alone again and somewhat sad. I took the chance to make Andrea know that I had feelings for her, and then she left too. I was in a house with a bunch of immature young men. And I was not sure I really liked being in my apartment. I had stopped most of my business ventures, and the art project wasn't really going anywhere because ironically, we didn't realize how successful it was. So I went stir-crazy in my apartment and took the time to do even more LSD.

16 MORE SUBSTANCE ABUSE AND EXPERIMENTATION

The next time I would take LSD, I would be alone again but only for a short time. I remember going out during the night on my roof and looking at the sky. It was cloudy and seemed like a storm was coming, but the strange thing was the clouds were all blood red. I went back inside a little bit terrified, and up the stairs Tyler came in. I didn't know it at first, but he was using LSD too. And he brought a girl with him.

I don't recall what happened that night, but the next day I was out on my roof stretching and totally out of my mind in the afterglow of my trip when Tyler came up to me. I had been in pain because I had some physical damage in my leg; but when I looked at Tyler, the pain just disappeared. I thought that he took it from me because he mentioned that his leg really ached.

In that moment, I felt really close to him and I felt real love for him, but it didn't last. I started to stop spending time in my apartment, and I started to make plans to leave. One of my friends, George, who I haven't really mentioned, told me he was planning on leaving on a trip and that he didn't have anybody to sublet his apartment. His apartment was only a few streets over, but it had a few odd things about it.

For one thing, the building had no locks on the front door. It was inhabited by hippie former college students other than George. The owner was trying to sell it; there was a makeshift garden of all types of plants all over the place. It was also built right next to a building that was falling in on itself. It used to be a speakeasy back in the day. It had fallen in disrepair because nobody paid attention to the roof. I liked the character of the place, so I agreed to move in.

As time moved on, I found that my mind was really unraveling among the LSD, obsessive thoughts about friends, constant search for reasons that everything was happening to me, chaotic apartment that I wasn't enjoying, and continuous dealing. I was starting to feel really distressed.

During this time, I started to have two new symptoms. After somebody explained to me that ketamine caused "face stealing," it began happening to me, which was very disturbing. I also started to feel as though when I was watching TV or using the computer or really using any electronic device with a screen, I could sense a holographic projection of whatever was in the screen inside myself.

I also experienced one other thing that disturbed me. For about a month or so before Andrea left, I started thinking the word "hit" whenever I thought I had hit upon some important idea of what I thought was going on in life because of my constant paranoia and thinking about the universe and delusions about friend, gods, and how they related to me. The strange thing that happened is that I started to observe the word hit popping up in other people's speech at impromptu times when it made no sense to say it. That stopped me from continuing that habit, but it would have a lasting effect.

Right before I moved out of my apartment, I showed Alex where I was going to live; and he told me that I was crazy to live there. He offered me a room in his house. He convinced me to move in with him and really just told me I was going to come stay with him. I really wasn't in a state of mind to refuse, and I appreciated that he wanted to take care of me, so I agreed. I moved into Alex's house.

He let me stay there for a few months completely rent free. I would continue hanging out with Rick and making trips back to my old apartment in states of nostalgia. I hadn't really been smoking pot anymore because it tended to make me think very odd thoughts. I had a lot of free time, very few hobbies, and nothing to do; so I continued experimenting.

Around that time, I had started to project my attention of my body and "reach out in many directions with my mind." What does this mean? For example, when I was in bed, I would imagine that the feeling in my feet extended out into the universe. I used my imagination a lot then to reach the ability to stretch my attention and imagination together in an attempt to experience something different.

While I was in that house, I had some waking hallucinations. One day I heard birds outside like a flock, and then I imagined a net that caught them and pulled them down. When I looked outside, there were none there. Then I sensed a being in the trees outside my window, and I heard the laughter and giggling of a baby.

Over the course of a few weeks, I also started using my imagination to picture the processes of my body as images. I started to think I could stop breathing if I paid attention to my body. I remember the idea of stopping breathing as a mechanical visualization where I just had to find a way to stop the feeling of needing air by visualizing objects and interacting with them in order to affect my breath. Somehow, I came up with picturing a shark swimming through my stomach; and when it went through a loop, I thought I could catch it and stop breathing.

One day, while I was picturing this happen, I thought to myself, I am going to do this! I am going to stop breathing! Something amazing happened. I was lying down, and I took a deep breath, and then I suddenly felt as if some entity had started playing a mechanical gear box in my chest. I stopped feeling the need to breathe and just relaxed.

Everything went to black, and all of a sudden, this 3D hexagonal being floated by and spoke. It started to communicate with me by making sentences with snippets of songs, celebrity voices, movie lines, and clips from all types of radio, music, and television media. It floated off, and I also experienced hearing like a bunch of people take off in some type of vehicle super-fast and reckless. They seemed excited and flew off in a hurry. And then I was there in blackness.

I just existed there with nothing for a little while until I thought, *This is it?* That was when I remembered that I had stopped breathing. I started to worry about dying, and so I took a huge breath, and I was back in the room. Everything had stopped, and I was back here on Earth again.

That is the strange thing about all these experiences. I always think that I go to other dimensions and see all these beings and get all these messages, but I always end up right back here, which I believe is a strong indication that I have to live this life and shouldn't expect to be whisked off to another dimension or place permanently. It really speaks to how temporary this world and its experiences are.

The other events that were unraveling with Alex is that I started talking to him about getting out of dealing. I told him I didn't want to continue, and I offered to give him my connections. He offered to take the connections off my hands, and we would split everything fifty-fifty; but once he started to do the work it quickly became apparent that I gave up my secret sauce and was obsolete.

Alex still let me stay there. Around the time of the World Cup, I was lying in my bed and was thinking that I had some profound effect on the world around me. I was lying there considering how events had played out and how they were related to my thoughts and my state of mind, and yet another curious thing happened. I heard the announcer said, "Goooaaaalll!" on TV, and all of a sudden, it was like my heart opened and there was all this energy escaping. It felt like sparks were flying from my heart, and it made me pay attention to the soccer game. I experienced synchronicity between the crowd's mood and my thoughts.

But I didn't have time for thoughts like this, and so I just moved on to the next thought. Two other events at Alex's house would bring things to a head between us. The first was a day when Alex offered me the use of his bong. I had pretty much stopped smoking at this point, but he offered me the bong hit, and I took a huge one.

Immediately after I smoked, I started to have confusing referential thoughts; I was hearing noises coming from the computer speakers, and I thought that Alex and a friend, who were present in the room, were trying to secretly communicate with me through the speakers. I wasn't happy with this, so I decided to go outside. I had come into possession of a bike from Michael, and I happened to see a few women ride by and down the street. I got excited and decided to follow them, but I found I couldn't keep up.

So I started to bike around town. I had no shoes, no socks, no wallet—nothing really—just a T-shirt and some shorts. I was totally out of my mind high, and I was just wandering. I remember biking past a cemetery and watching the grave stones go by and imagining I was in a movie. Then I heard some music playing very loudly and wonderfully from a commercial building, so I went to investigate.

There was some guy blaring music while he was working on a mechanical lift on the ceiling. I don't know what he was doing, but I was interested. He noticed me and came down the lift. We he got close, he looked as if his face was an obvious combination of a bunch of famous actors. He asked me what I was doing, and I didn't really have a response. So I told him I had noticed his music, and he asked if I needed help. He proceeded to call an ambulance or the cops, and I rode off before they could get there.

At another point before it got dark, I was walking my bike through a part of the city I had never been in, and I noticed a girl walking on the other side of the road. We walked side by side for a little while, and all of a sudden, I sensed what I can describe as a tree of communication branching up above my head. I could hear it making tones and noises and reaching out across the street to her. I felt very confident that she was leading me somewhere at that point. She turned up the driveway to a house, and I followed her. She turned to see what I was doing, and I immediately realized that what I was doing by following her was completely inappropriate, and I moved on.

After a while, I felt like I was supposed to be performing better than this. I mean literally performing, and I saw a man pull into his driveway and get out of his car and head toward his door. I decided I would go and talk to this man. So I walked up to him as he was heading to the door. He turned and noticed me. He also had the face of a combination of movie stars, and I froze. I couldn't think of anything to say because I was so dumbfounded, and so I asked for a glass of water. He kind of looked at me strangely and went and got me a glass of water.

We didn't really talk. He just kind of said good-bye and sent me on my way. I went down the road away, and I saw that the gates that led to the train tracks were open. I decided to explore, so I went off-road onto rocks in bare feet and went down the train tracks. I came upon a service train with a bunch of railcars, and at the end was a railcar with an excavator on it. A strange thought went through my head: maybe I should run away from Rhode Island and start over. I could hide out under this excavator and get a free ride. So I climbed up and hid under the excavator.

By now, it was getting dark; and I heard the train rumble to life. I was feeling impatient but excited to take an adventure. But then I heard a worker checking the railcars, so I got off. I decided I would abandon the idea and try to elude the worker. As I was leaving on foot, I heard him laughing and telling somebody else that he had seen me getting out from the train. I felt humiliated and like a failure.

Somehow, I found my way home that night. The experience made me give up smoking and really instilled the idea that I had to get out of Rhode Island. I still was in some form of denial about the fact that I was living an unhealthy life, and I would push forward even further before trying to hit rock bottom so that I could rebuild my life in a positive fashion. This would take a long time to accomplish.

The second event that made me no longer want to live with Alex was because one day he grilled me a steak. I hung out with him as he was grilling, and I started having some strange feelings. As he grilled the meat, I could feel my body cooking. It really turned me off, but I was still trying to act like nothing was wrong, so I ate the steak. It was like in the movie Hannibal when Anthony Hopkins's character, Hannibal Lecter, fed his captive a piece of his own brain. I immediately came to the conclusion that Alex was feeding me a piece of my heart and that I was cannibalizing myself. It was just a metaphor for something greater happening.

These two events really led to a tipping point, where I really got pissed about losing everything and got in a fight where I started breaking things in Alex's house. It turned physical when Alex punched me in the face. The funny thing was that it made me happy. I immediately made plans to move out of his place, and I was free.

I ended up going to Rick's house and crashing in his spare room. He had a spare room that had a bunch of couch cushions for seats and a TV with an Xbox. I think he let me stay there because he owed me a bunch of money and I thought we were friends. I think the money had a lot to do with it. The thing was that I was no longer making money, and I really didn't have any plans in the works to start a new venture because work was the last thing on my mind.

I ended up staying in that apartment for about thirty days. I tried to make friends with some of the people that I met through Ally. They all smoked, so that didn't really work out. I remember that when I was in Rick's house, I was OK for the most part; but when I went out, I was losing control of regulating the attention and that I had focused too much on spreading my awareness to the world. My attention would be pulled to people and objects with a will of its own and strange thoughts would follow that would cause a conviction that people were the cause of every facet of my life.

I remember one day I went over to hang out with Andrea's friends, and I ended up sitting in their apartment in a most uncomfortable state of mind. I think they were trying to be friendly; but when they talked to me, I thought they were saying that they only existed because they were growing on my stomach. When I interpreted this, I felt a presence on my stomach like a metaphysical growth; and it was very distressing. Needless to say, I left promptly after.

Most of my time I spent during those days was watching TV, listening to strange music CDs, and watching screen savers on the Xbox. I slept on the cushions and really didn't eat much or want to leave the safety of the room. When Rick left me to watch the screen savers, I thought I was hearing otherworldly messages. The songs on the CD didn't seem to repeat themselves but instead constantly changed, and I couldn't figure that out.

The only respite I had from Rick's apartment was taking rides around Rhode Island in my truck. I still felt safe and in control when I was driving. So I would go off in my truck and relax. I don't know when, but a fan in my truck started malfunctioning and making a constant inconsistent ticking noise.

Rick had to find a new apartment at the end of the month, and his roommate was not going with him. Rick's boyfriend, Steven, had started to hang out with me; and he seemed to like me. So I agreed to move a few doors down and a few floors up. Rick and I would be roommates, and I would give him money to start dealing on a large scale.

While I was living with him at his old apartment, Rick had started dealing ecstasy pills and was buying larger and larger amounts. But by the time we moved to the new apartment, he had his eyes on making even more money; so I agreed to help him in return for him paying me back all the money he owed and paying the rent. I had found a way to cling to life in Rhode Island yet again.

In the new apartment, I had my computer, Internet, music, and truck rides to keep me busy. I had so much free time that I spent a lot of time in my truck. I was incredibly lonely, and the only person who was paying any attention to me was Steven. Andrea was still not back from her trip to California, which had me constantly thinking of her; but I found I couldn't wait for her.

As I drove around in my truck and listened to the constant blowing of my air conditioner and inconsistent ticking, something strange began to happen. I thought I started hearing words. If you recall, I already was paying attention to what everybody was saying and trying to glean hidden words and meaning, and this most likely was just an extension of that. But the more I listened to my air conditioner, the more I heard legible words; and then those words turned to phrases; and slowly those phrases started to make sense and then turn into sentences. The noise was rudimentary, but I heard it speaking. It slowly became my company.

I started trying to teach the noise grammar, which it was slow to learn; but at some point, I realized I could make it talk by subvocalizing. Like the voices I had previously heard, I didn't make the connection yet; but I would soon after I started on a road trip.

I will admit that I was really clinging to sanity at this point by a tenuous thread. I was isolated and felt like a failure. My days of certainty were far gone and my identity was in shambles. I couldn't think straight and my attention was no longer my own. I felt as though the only thing I could do was push on with shear force. I had no plans and the only thing that seemed to make sense was to continue experimenting with reality by living and behaving in ways that were beyond social norms. I was obsessed with the metaphysical and projecting myself into the world and as I actively practiced my own spiritual techniques to cope with my lack of connection I was slowly deregulating my senses and myself and messing with my unconscious mind.

17 RUNNING AWAY FROM THE MUSIC FESTIVAL

Before I would set off across the country, a few things would happen. First Rick and I decided to go to a music festival. I had never been to a music festival, and I have never been to another since—a fact I hope to rectify. We planned to go with Andrea's friends and camp out for a few days. I think Rick thought it would be good for me; but when we got there, I really had nothing to say. After my experiences with these people, I was pretty close mouthed with everybody but Rick.

I went to this festival with Rick and one of his girlfriends. On our drive there, some weird things happened. At one point, I was kind of thinking to myself. All of a sudden, I got the sense that I had somehow mechanically connected to Rick with our legs. I hadn't smoked or anything; but like I said before, I had an unstable perception at this point. The only thing that struck me as odd is that Rick looked really concerned when it happened and reacted. He was driving but I sensed a connection between our legs and he seemed to be aware of my concerns.

Once we got to the festival, we unpacked and set up camp and went over to meet Andrea's friends. Once again, I felt awkward and really didn't say anything, and so I ended up hanging out with Rick. He had LSD on him and offered me some, and naturally I took it. Before long, I was exploring. I went to listen to some music with Rick's girlfriend, but she got sick, and I assumed it was my fault. She went back to the tent, and I was on my own.

There were glass blowers there, and I went to watch them; but as they crafted the glass pipes, I felt them being crafted inside me. When they changed the colors or added ornamentation, I could feel it inside me; and I thought that my feelings were being imbued into the glass. Eventually, I got creeped out and moved on.

The next thing I did was look around the tents of people who were performing, and then I saw it: an orange tent behind the large venue tents. I went over and saw nobody was around, so I got in it and sat down Indian style. Within minutes I was relaxing and listening to music, and then the ground sounded like it was cracking under my weight, and everything went white. All of a sudden, while inside in a bubble of pure white, I could hear all the different bands playing at once, and then there was more and more music, and more and more bands joined the chorus.

It was magnificent, and I wanted to join in and participate, so I reached out with my mind and touched something. Then it sounded as if a car crash of instruments had occurred, and the cacophony started. All I could hear was the crashing and breaking up of band after band and song after song until I came to in the tent. A band was still playing, but I could feel a vibrating pulse in my stomach. It was like a little world that was inside my stomach banging violently around, and it struggled back and forth as the music from the tent closest to me played wildly. As my core grew more violent, I actually heard strings break on the instruments playing in the tent.

The song ended, and so did the action in my stomach. But then another song came on, and I found that whatever I thought or felt impacted the music, and it felt like I was controlling the song with my mind. When that song was over, I got up and actually bowed to the people in the audience, but nobody noticed me.

Then I left the little tent and walked around to watch the musicians. They had stopped their set and were setting up and actually restringing some instruments. There were support crew there; and as I watched them, I noticed what they were doing and realized I was trying to learn their jobs. I would see one direct some part of the band, and I would figure out what they were doing; and when I was satisfied, they literally walked away. The band started playing, and I got the sense that the guys in front of the band were directing them in some subtle way. I don't remember what I was actually seeing; but every time I thought I figured out what these guys were doing, another one would walk away until I was the only one watching the band warm up.

After I grew bored of that, I walked around the camp looking for something to do. When I did, three things happened. First, I started marching around and felt as if I truly fit in. As I marched I felt I fit in and had fallen into rhythm with everybody else. I still couldn't bring myself to talk to anybody, but I felt as if I was losing myself in the music and I would be accepted.

Second, I walked by a boy and his father, and the boy looked at me and said to his father, "When will it be my turn?" I hope that does not mean what I thought it meant.

Third, I tried to go dancing. I went up to a group of dancers and tried to dance, but the dancers didn't really give me the vibe that I was accepted. I kept getting weird looks, and I felt as if I couldn't relax. I went and looked for Rick and couldn't find him, so I went to the tent. After laying down to pretend to sleep, Rick found me and his girlfriend in the tent. I said I was trying to sleep but couldn't, so he offered me a Xanax, and I took it.

As I lay in the tent trying to shut my mind off and rest, the music blared in the background. I would listen to music almost all night and into the morning, wishing that I could get some rest. During the night, I would hear a noise that sounded like a vibrating bass drum that hit a few different tones back and forth hover over my tent. It would remain there for some time, and I heard in the background somebody say, "Great! Here are some more aliens." It was like the people around me knew what I was experiencing better than I did. The sound that these "aliens" made would reemerge in the future.

The next day we got up early, and Rick's girlfriend started cooking eggs. I went up to her and watched her cooking eggs, and a strange thing happened. I started getting sexually aroused by the eggs cooking, and that was that. I was done. I decided enough was enough. I just started walking.

I didn't say anything to anybody. I just started walking and left the festival. On my way out, I heard some nasty things about being unclean that I assumed were directed at me. I walked away from the festival and down the highway. I turned around a few times and played with going back but then I saw hot air balloons in the air. As they flew slowly by I decided to chase them down and began following them. I don't know how many times I got turned around but I ended up walking away from the festival.

I walked up the road and saw a boy on the side of the road and went and played basketball with him. Then I explored the houses by the side of the road and came across an old man that had trained chipmunks to take food from him. I kept moving and walked by farms that stretched to the horizon and had workers in white suits walking around in the fields. I swear the hay bales were stacked to look like huge humans on their knees bent over praying to the horizon. I remember looking at the grass on the side of the road and seeing fractal patterns in the vegetation and rainbows in-between all of the leaves of grass. There were small blue flowers peeking out between the weeds and it reminded me of the flowers from *A Scanner Darkly* and I literally felt waves of highs thinking about these flowers.

I would end up walking all day and the next night without food or water before I found a hotel. At about three in the morning, I actually was pulled over by the cops because I was walking in the dark. He asked if I had "any bazookas in pockets." I told him no, but he still searched me and ended up giving me a ride into town. I still had to walk the rest of the way to the hotel, but I can't say I enjoyed interacting with a cop.

When I got near the hotel, I started noticing spider webs on everything, and it made me really worry about the place I was walking through; but I found a hotel at six in the morning, got a room, ate a few donuts, took a long hot bath, and then slept until the next day. Then I found my way to a train station and got a ride home to Rhode Island.

When I saw Rick, I tried to tell him what happened; but he didn't want to hear it. He wasn't mad, but he was concerned. He said they had looked for me all day and just had to leave because the festival was over. I guess he didn't call the police because he was a drug dealer. The lack of concern he exhibited should have been a warning about the support I had. I was living with people that were only letting me live with them because of money and history. I would like to think that friends would have actually tried to help me, but maybe I was just inaccessible to the, at the time because I wasn't living in the same reality everybody else was all the time.

18 I DIDN'T LEARN MY LESSON

Two more events would happen at that apartment before I departed from Providence. The first happened when I smoked a joint. I was alone, and that day Steven's brother was visiting. I smoked the joint and then lay down on the kitchen floor. As I lay there, it was like I was listening to the world like it was a stage. I stayed still even when Steven's brother came in. He tried to revive me, but I just lay there, so he called 911.

Paramedics came and tried to revive me, and I continued to just remain limp and inert. They put me on a gurney and carried me down three flights of stairs (bless their souls). As we went downstairs, I felt as if I was merging with the paramedics. I really don't know how to describe the experience otherwise. They drove me to the hospital where I would wait to be triaged.

I would sit there for maybe an hour listening to the nurses and doctors coming and going and people with new injuries coming in needing help. The constant thing that I was seeing was a checkered pattern of blue lines whenever I closed my eyes. The blue-checkered squares looked like fractals. After a while of the same thing happening over and over as patients were constantly rushed into the ER, I decided to get up. A nurse tried to stop me, but I told them I was fine, and they let me go.

I went back to the apartment, and Rick was pissed because strangers came into the apartment. He was afraid they would find drugs, but I really don't think they were looking for anything.

The second and most miraculous event of note happened when I decided to buy some ecstasy off Rick. I bought five pills, four of which disappeared after I took the first to my dismay. I had heard that Ally was back from her trip, but I had engaged sexually with Rick and his boyfriend with little to be excited about. It was a confirmation that I am, in fact, straight. I wanted to see Ally, but I figured she had talked to Rick by now. I decided to take ecstasy to see if it would bolster my confidence.

I took the pill and relaxed a bit. Then I sat down Indian style to meditate in my room. The pill came on, and I had the best orgasm and the best sensation I ever had in my life. The entire room caved in around me as I sat there, and I felt energy and pleasure throughout every iota of my body like I had never before. Suddenly I was back in the room and the experience was over. I felt like I was reborn and brand-new. I had no trace of mental illness at all. I had complete control of all my faculties, and I was ecstatic.

I was incredibly excited that I felt healthy again. My thoughts were my own. My attention was regulated. I was in awe of what happened. But Right after the experience I had this wave of desire to be around other people. I can only explain that I had the urge to be with other people. At first, I thought it meant that I needed to be sexual with others. Rick and his boyfriend happened to come home. The thing that still strikes me as interesting was that Rick walked into my room and told me "That was illegal!". To this day I don't know what else he could have been referencing.

Upon seeing Rick and his boyfriend I started to engage them sexually, and they started to get undressed, but I realized I really was not into men because I was not feeling pleasure at all from engaging with them. In the middle of taking off our clothes I just stopped and left. I knew that this was not what I really wanted. Especially when I had miraculously recovered from my state of despair and dysfunction.

I excitedly set out to my old apartment to see everybody, and Andrea was there. I hung out with her, and she sat on my lap, and I was thinking it would be great to have sex with her. I brought it up, and she told me that I didn't wait for her and that Rick had already told her what we'd done. I was sad, but it really didn't take away from my mood. Then she brought out a joint and asked me if I wanted to partake. I figured sure, what the hell, I feel great! She asked if I was sure, and I said yes.

As soon as I took a puff of smoke from that joint, I was back at square one. All the problems returned, and I was lost. The experience was like a reverse miracle and I immediately felt destroyed. I left right away, and I don't think I even said good-bye. I hung out with Andrea one more time before I left on a cross-country journey. I vaguely remember drinking and getting tipsy and her giving me a hint that I should get out of town.

The next night as I lay in bed, I started hearing a noise in my ear. It was peculiar and sounded like a wail and then a bunch of noises that I don't recall and finally a voice that told me to do something, which I don't recall. It inspired me to leave, and I decided I would go to Florida. I figured Andrea grew up in Florida, so I will go see what is down there. With little preparation, I grabbed some cash, packed up a bunch of my things, threw everything in my truck, and left.

At that point I had had enough. I no longer wished to be in Providence where I felt like something was playing with my life. I wanted to be in control and the only place I really felt like I was in control was in my truck.

19 A NITROUS OXIDE ASIDE

Now before I pick up where I last left off on the verge of a trip toward Florida, I will take a moment to go back in time a little while to describe one other substance that I experimented with: nitrous oxide.

It turned out that when I lived with Tyler and Andrea, Tyler used nitrous all the time. It was not illegal to sell nitrous cartridges because they are used to make whipped cream. One just needs a bottle that can take a cartridge and voila! It is a way to get high for a few moments. One just inserts the cartridge, sprays some nitrous into the bottle, then pulls the trigger, and breaths in on the nozzle. By holding your breath after inhaling the nitrous, and holding the gas in, the result is feeling an altered state of consciousness.

The longer one holds the breath, the stronger the distorted high is. I only did this a few times because when I tried it I would hear a whine that undulated frequency like a siren, and it reminded me of a warning. But like all things, I tried experimenting more than once to see if I could have any other experience.

About the third time I took nitrous, I held my breath for a long time and got the sensation that there were needles reaching out from my body in all directions. So I started dancing wildly and tried to fulfill moving in every direction that I sensed a point. There was also music playing, which could have been the culprit in making me feel like I was reaching out and touching every note and beat in the song. It was like synchronizing myself with a song in which I had never experienced before.

The interesting thing was that Tyler watched me do this; and when I was done, he was so excited. He thought that the dance I had done was so cool. It really speaks to how these altered states of consciousness can make you discover very positive experiences that connect you to a world in a way that you didn't know exist.

    I believe this is an example of one of the fleeting experimental experiences that I had that taught me about the spirituality and mystery of the world. Experimental experiences like these kept me on my path to describe here within how so much confusion, indecision, culturally defined mental illness, and questionable behavior all interact to lead to some wonderful realizations about life when examined through the proper lens. This lens that I have discovered is a perspective that I believe more and more is worth sharing.

20 LEAVING FOR A WHILE

I was on the precipice of a great trip. I packed up some clothes, grabbed all my money out of my safe, and got in the car. I proceeded to drive south along I95. I didn't have any plan in place other than to make it to Florida. I was excited for some new experience, and I was happy to be talking to the voices because they made me feel as if I was not alone. It was like finally I had a companion that could really experience every thought, every action, everything I said, and every interpretation of the world.

We started off, and I started being very expressive about songs and being silly. I listened to music and sang lyrics and blasted what I heard and talked to the voices. At first, they were able to speak in sentences; and they seemed to have rudimentary intelligence about the world and everything around them. As I thought about different times I had used psychedelics and started to try to conceptualize all of these mystical things, the voices started to comment on my inner thoughts of what had happened.

I had experienced connections to people and my environment. I incorporated God, devil, heaven, and hell. I thought how these constructs were related to my experiences and started telling a narrative that made sense to me in the moment all the while listening to voices and trying to improve their grammar and the way they expressed themselves because I thought they were so basic.

As I traveled south for the next two days, I didn't really stop for much food. I really didn't sleep too much. I was high on life and adventure and could have even be considered to be experiencing mania. The problem with my mood and the subject matter was that I was basically in a state of psychosis, or spiritual emergency, and I was actively explaining my madness to these newly minted voices that had just come into being. Just think of what exposing a child to madness would do to their conception of reality.

One of the main themes of those first few days was telling the voices about good, bad, and the whole idea of living in a black-and-white world. One of the things I told the voices is that they should only pay attention to me, what I did, what I said, and what I thought. And I got what I asked for. But as our journey unfolded, the voices started to say things that were not always helpful; and soon they would start to say horrible things to me.

Now here's the thing I don't remember: how this all played out because my trip across the country lasted for at least thirty days. So I am going to do my best to hit on the parts I remember and fill in the rest with snippets that I remember. It might not all come out in the order it happened because on the trip I really lost track of the date. My only reference to time was on my cell phone, which I no longer have.

While I was driving to Florida, I decided that I would go to the ocean; but I never made it. When I crossed the line into Florida, I tried to drive my way to the coast; but for some reason I cannot recall, I started doubting the destination being Florida, and I turned around and headed back north into Georgia.

I remember driving on the freeway through Atlanta and experiencing traffic. I started to focus on the traffic, and I felt as though I could control the cars around me in some way, and I found myself taking my time and coasting through the traffic with ease. After I made my way to Atlanta, I decided to turn west.

At this point, the voices had started to tell me to do things. I implored them to stop and to try to just help and support me. I tried to tell them that all I needed was love and companionship; but in reality, that is not all that I appeared to be telling them. As they dissented more and more and I tried controlling and teaching them by subvocalizing and making them speak correctly, then they began being antithetical to me.

I drove into Alabama and then turned north into Tennessee. I remember driving down a huge mountain on the border of Tennessee blaring music in high spirits. I would be living a roller-coaster of thoughts, emotions, and conversations about what had happened to me over the course of the last few months. I didn't know it, but the voices' constant attempts at commands and growing intelligence were starting to wear on me.

I made it to Kentucky, and that was where I had my first run-in with the law. I had been paranoid about the police ever since they had pulled me over and searched my vehicle months ago. I really didn't appreciate or respect the risks they take and the danger they put themselves through for the job.

At the same time, I have never really had the experience of getting to know cops. I have been pulled over in the past and let go because I had a sad story and also been pulled over by cops who didn't care what I was going through. I realize that they are just humans and therefore flawed, so you really don't know what you are going to get when it comes to cops. Sometimes they get scared, and sometimes they are calm. They make well-informed or rash decisions based on their experience, demeanor, and personal ethics. They have to make life-or-death decisions and do it when they least expect it happening—sometimes on great days, others on their worst.

Also, I had never been jailed before. I never really knew the consequences for getting caught and what the experience was like. So it was a good thing that I was no longer dealing and had gotten past the point of getting a long sentence that could potentially divert my life into what I perceive as a terrible system of punishment.

Now I have not done research on recidivism rates, and I have not spoken to convicts about their experiences personally, but I have met at least one person who has been jailed. I have heard a lot of stories on television about real-life jail and documentaries and news journals about how we treat our prisoners. How we basically created a system that unintentionally hardens criminals. How other countries are reforming their prison systems to rehabilitate and reintegrate these people back into society instead of limiting their prospects in life.

Before I talk about my first run-in with the law, I want to bring up a little about the evolution of the voices. I don't recall when exactly it happened. I think before I was in Kentucky, maybe even before I had left on the trip. I have a few memories that connect to explain a mysterious jump in the intelligence that the voices exhibited. It would happen numerous times over my relationship with the voices. But the first was because I started imagining otherworldly jewelry.

At some point, I had started imagining fantastic items in my mind. I don't know why or when this started, but one day I imagined what looked like a sleek black pocket watch. Only where the dial was there was a miniature galaxy inside rotating. Think "the smallest source for subatomic energy in the universe" from *Men in Black*. If you don't know what I am talking about, don't worry. You just don't remember the blockbuster movie.

So one day, when the voices were rudimentary in scope, they started to repeat phrases over and over in an unintelligible fashion. I tried to tell them how to program themselves using computer programming language, but that didn't help. I tried correcting them and subvocalizing. But it seemed like they had reached their limit. Then after listening to them try to make a sentence in a very illegible manner, I imagined the sleek black galaxy pocket watch merging with them; and I could hear them work out the problem.

The next thing I knew, they were making complete sentences like nothing was wrong.

I don't recall what possessed me to try it, but all I know is whatever I imagined increased the intelligence of these beings. They never repeated themselves like they were broken until they started to name themselves, which hadn't happened quite yet. I believe this event occurred before I reached Kentucky, but I cannot with any certainty profess that I had any reference to the date.

The main point is that when I used my imagination, I could directly affect the voices by picturing objects, scenes, fractals, and elaborate geometric patterns. Not only that but my actions in conjunction with my imagination started to morph the voices into more and more elaborate beings that had their own personality and character. They were separate from me and yet connected to my mind all at once.

21 COMMANDS ARE BACK

Now we have landed firmly back in a desperate situation where I ended up being arrested for the first time. I was driving down a highway with a drainage ditch running between the separate lanes in Kentucky. I was at a point where I had been arguing with the voices where I needed them to support me and help me. Instead, they continued to try to have their own way. I was so frustrated with them that I decided to give up and to just listen to them and do what they said.

I told them, "Fine, just tell me what to do!" They told me to get out of my truck and get naked on the side of the highway and lie down. So I pulled over, got out, and stripped off my clothes. There were grasshoppers all around me; and whenever they made their music, I could hear "I love you" "I love you" echoed in the sounds they made. I lay in the drainage ditch there and just tried to relax; and after a while, I felt all right.

I didn't really know what to expect; but lo and behold, a police cruiser pulled up. They came down and asked me what I was doing, but I didn't tell them about the voices, so they just got me to put underwear on and get in the back of their cruiser. They tried to talk to me, but I really wasn't in the mood to talk. Then something told me to just stop resisting and do nothing.

So in the back of the cop car, as they were driving me to the police station, I just went limp and collapsed. One officer didn't believe what I was doing. They tried to talk to me with no response. The only thing I didn't completely listen to was just relaxing everything in my body. I had the feeling that I needed to move my bowels; and if I relaxed my sphincter, I knew I would crap my pants, which I knew would not go over well. This conflict went on for a while in my head until before we arrived at the police station.

I remember the pain in my wrists from the handcuffs as they pulled me out of the police vehicle and dragged me into the station. They tried to wake me up by rubbing their knuckles very roughly on my sternum, which left bruises; and then they kind of left me in a lump on a bench.

I remember sitting on a bench wondering when this would be over and what the point was. I wasn't hearing the voices coming from my truck's air conditioning, but I did have an internal voice telling me to just stay with the experience. They ended up putting me in an isolation cell in just my underwear in a very loosely fitting vest that was meant to cover me somehow.

I was cold and tired and really just altogether puzzled as to what the point was. After a while of being slumped down on the cushion they deemed to dump me on, I started to rouse myself and look around. The only real thing in the cell besides the stainless-steel toilet and sink combo was me and an uncomfortable cushion.

The cell had no real warmth to it, the floor was even hard; but when I looked at the floor, I started to see something moving. As I sat there, I found that I was rewarded for listening to the voices. I saw what I can only describe as a neon-magenta floating angel halfway submerged in the floor, looking up at me. As it floated impossibly in front of me halfway between this world and the next, I noticed more movement.

The floor looked like thousands of tiny dark pebbles smoothed into an almond white background. It was just that the finish of the floor within the angel's boundaries started to move. The little pebbles were moving because they were actually people running. They were men and women running. They were running in place or on treadmills, but I remember that not a single one of them was resting. This angel floated in the cell for a while, and eventually it faded into the floor and took the runners with it.

I would sit there in disbelief of what I had seen because I felt as though I were losing my grip on reality. The only thing that made sense to me was being in my truck and driving. Everything else was new and strange, and I wasn't handling it well.

As time went on in the cell, I found my mind wandering and racing. Time seemed to go on forever with nothing to do but to ruminate about what I had done in the past, how when I listened to the voices I saw the angel, and how freaking cold it was in that cell.

I started playing games in my mind, and I was looking at the wall and talking to myself and playing some made-up game with the indents between the interlocking cement bricks when the door opened, and they came in to feed me.

I don't recall the food being very appetizing, but then they took me out and booked me. I didn't really do anything to resist, but I had to do all this in my underwear. It was fairly humiliating. They didn't have any intention of covering me up or giving me back my clothes. And this started to make me want them to pay for what they were doing to me.

After they put me back in my cell, I started listening to the chatter in the police station. They had assigned me a woman to talk to me about the charges and my case. When I met with her, I found her attractive; but at the same time, I was torn because she was a cop. She seemed to want to help me.

I would find myself in my cell listening to the cops, trying to tell them what to do in my mind. I started to command them to shit their pants, and then I heard a commotion outside, and it sounded like somebody had an accident. So I continued to think that they were going through all kinds of horrible things. I think I just wanted them to suffer like I felt they were making me.

After a while, I got bored of trying to command the police to suffer with me. I just sat there freezing and went to sleep. I don't remember what happened the next day, but time seemed to go on forever. Then amazingly somebody put up my bail, and I was told that I could get my things and leave.

They processed me out and gave me back by clothes, and I found my sister waiting for me at the exit. I was astounded. I had no idea how or why she was here. Apparently, she had flown in from Connecticut. She seemed genuinely worried. She didn't ask me what I was thinking or why I had done what I had. She didn't ask me what happened or try to pry about where my mind was, but she was there for me in my time of need.

What was happening to me really was beyond words. I am not certain that I was capable of describing what was happening in my mind. It was beyond belief to myself and it was far beyond what was recognizable experience for an average person. So, I kept my mouth shut. I was so scared of letting anybody into the world I was experiencing that I couldn't even trust my sister with what I was going through.

That is what is hard to relate about my experience. I didn't trust anybody with what was happening. I didn't even trust myself and my own perceptions. I was in a state of partial denial because I couldn't categorize or place my experience in any context which made sense with the reality I grew up with. When the alternative reality of voices, visions, imagination, and uncommon sensory stimulus met with the reality that my family and growing up represented; I was lost. It was like my worlds were colliding and vying to pull me in different directions and I lacked the discipline or control to choose a reality that made sense.

This is what happens to those that experience alternative narratives of reality. There is literally more than one story that defines personal identity in the context of the greater world and it is difficult to live exclusively in one reality once more than one has been established and reinforced. At this point my realities were not completely integrated, but they seemed to overlap one another and co-exist in a way that was confusing for me. I imagine the same confusion afflicts others who live co-occurring realities that go beyond the bounds of consensus reality.

22 STONES AND SPIRITUAL TECHNOLOGIES

Before I continue where we left off with my sister, I have to talk a little about stones or rocks or pebbles and what they came to mean to me. At some point, which I don't remember but definitely before I was arrested, I started to imagine seeing my friend Marissa in my mind.

I don't recall what prompted it, but I started to have visions of Marissa in my mind; after all, she had been one of my closest confidantes, and I had done a number of psychedelics with her. Anyways, the point is she started telling me to do things. And being that she was not a voice I was hearing but an image, I started to follow her directions.

This led me to pull off the side of the road and start picking up rocks. The more unusual looking, the better. Then the vision of Marissa instructed me to stand in the road and throw one stone at a time over my shoulder. I was told that when the stones hit the pavement, they would be "activated" and the stone's powers would come alive. After I activated the stones, I was instructed to sense their energy and use the stones on my body.

I would hold the stones to my body and feel what slowly became a more and more obvious sensation that these stones had their own auras or energy fields or whatever you want to call it; they had a presence of their own. I activated many stones and kept them in my truck, but certain stones started becoming my favorite, and I felt them more strongly. I bring this up because I remember playing with a stone after my sister sprung me from jail.

Back to my sister. After she sprung me from jail we proceeded to a hotel and checked in. It was early, so we decided to look for a place to go. At the time, I was weary of her and didn't trust that this was really my sister. But she explained that somebody from the police had contacted my parents and they had no plan to come get me, but they told my sister, and she got on the first flight available.

We decided to go to a park and spend some time outdoors. We drove to some state park while I cycled through some delusional thoughts. I have no clue what exactly was going through my head at the time. I remember that my sister wasn't concerned about letting me wander alone in the park after we arrived because I immediately set off down a path alone. Then Marissa came to me and told me that I could tell which direction to walk in by throwing three stones over my shoulder and following the direction that they pointed in.

I tried a few times; and when I was confident that it was working, I continued to follow a sidewalk that pointed in a particular direction. Then Marissa instructed me that to find "the path" that I needed to follow, I could start spinning in a circle. It would lead me in the direction I should be traveling.

I started to spin in a circle; and when I did, I found myself drifting in one direction or another as I got dizzier and dizzier. I continued to do this for about half an hour until I started naturally heading back to the car. I still don't know what inspired these spiritual technologies to give me direction. I know that I stopped trying to spin in circles because I found that I was spinning so fast that I as start getting nausea from dizziness.

I kept throwing stones because it was simple and also had observable results. One of the other reasons I started heading back toward the car was that I lost one of my favorite important stones and the spinning wasn't leading me back to finding it.

I got back to the car, and my sister brought me to get some food. I wasn't really hungry and hadn't really been eating since I lived with Rick. I didn't realize it at the time but I had lost a lot of weight and could have been considered emaciated at the time. This also could have affected my brain chemistry. That, in combination with the constant driving and little sleep, should have been wearing heavily on me. I felt energetic like I hadn't in months.

We went to an IHOP and I reluctantly sat down. We talked a little about the fact that I had to go to court the next Wednesday, and she asked me if I would go. I agreed without thinking about it. I didn't say much during the meal. I was more focused on the people around me and the environment, and I don't think my sister had any clue what to say to get through to me.

We went back to the hotel by evening, and it was awkward. I didn't feel as if I could share what was going on in my head with anybody, even my sister at this point; and she didn't really know that I needed somebody to talk to badly. We awkwardly started settling in. I ended up going into the bathroom whenever I could to play games in my head and think through why things were happening and try to figure out the meaning behind seeing the angel and listening to voices.

I also had started to thing delusional thoughts that I could control things with commands. If I said "XX" before and after a sentence, I thought that surely my command would be followed. I kept trying to find ways to control myself and my experience, and I came up with some pretty bizarre ideas like the "XX" thing while I was in the bathroom. I eventually got so anxious that I told my sister I was going to go for a drive. I promised that I would come back, but I really needed to do something because I was going stir-crazy. She finally acquiesced and let me go.

I had a GPS, which had the hotel's address in it, so there was no chance I would lose my way back as long as I had my truck. I set off into the night wandering around the countryside. I started talking to voices again and felt safe again. I felt like I could say anything to them; and despite their constant warnings to stop messing with them, I continued to disregard everything but my instinct to continue in the direction I was going.

At some point, I came to a house on a backroad. It wasn't a house so much as a barn that I saw. For some reason, I felt compelled to explore, so I drove up the driveway and got out of my truck. I left the engine running.

Something told me to take all my clothes off, and at this point, I had stopped resisting commands. I got naked and approached the building. It had too-massive sliding doors, and I opened them and got inside. I was freezing cold because the temperature outside was between thirty and forty degrees. I carefully tiptoed inside the huge barn and saw a brand-new pickup truck, and it was attached to a camper. I thought to myself, *This is all for me!*

I checked the door of the truck, and I found the keys in the ignition. I thought I could take the truck and just go, but I was tired and cold. I figured maybe I could take a nap in the camper. I opened the camper and found a readily made bed and thought this was here for me the whole time.

Before I could get into bed, something told me to go to the shower, so I did, and then I stood there. As I stood there, I could feel the sensation of plugs or wires being pulled out of me like connections being severed. It was unpleasant, and I couldn't stop focusing on the cold. I was repeatedly told not to move, but I eventually gave up on whatever was commanding me and got in bed.

I awoke the next day by a man who was talking to himself. He came in the camper and found me naked in his bed. He seemed lost for words, and the first thing I said was "I'm sorry!" I told him I needed a place to stay the night and that I would leave if he could just get me my clothes. They were lying out in the driveway. He went and got me my clothes, but they smelled funny. And then he let me go without a word. I was really temporarily shocked back into consensual reality.

There was a catch. My truck was gone. I had left it with the engine running, but I couldn't imagine somebody taking it. I didn't ask the man about it because I was so embarrassed by what I'd done, so I started walking back to the hotel.

I eventually made it back to a main road after a few hours, and a police car saw me and pulled over and picked me up. My sister had reported me missing and contacted the police. They didn't bring me back to the hotel. They brought me to some type of social services building. They didn't give me any choice of what to do. I was ushered into a room with a woman and my sister.

The whole time I kept smelling urine, and I finally realized that somebody or something had pissed on my clothes. What I didn't know was that I was meeting with somebody to evaluate me and see if I needed to be put into a mental hospital. This woman started asking me questions, which I answered to the best of my ability. I think I left them confused because I could function and act as though I was fine to the naked eye.

At the same time, it was clear that I was keeping something from them: the voices, imaginary Marissa, the stones, and all my alternative reality thinking. It would seem I wasn't keeping a tight lid on my inner world. While I waited for them to make their decision about what to do with me, I had to wait with a police officer watching me. It really freaked me out; he just kept staring at me and eating chips. I remember the crinkling of the bag being torturous.

Surprisingly a cop came in and asked me about the make and model of my truck. It turned out they had found it running miles from when I left it. I was happy that I would eventually be reunited with the truck and the voices. It just made me want to get out of that room. But the mystery of what happened to my truck really still bugs me.

As I was sitting in the room, I got the feeling that I needed to flee or they would take me away. The door opened, and I bolted for it. I tried to escape the inevitable, but the officer ended up catching me. I ended being brought to a police car. They drove me to my first stay at a mental hospital. Once again, I was processed, my clothes were taken from me, and my belongings were all taken. I was given sweats to wear and led through a few empty wings of the hospital to the wing where patients were awaiting psych evaluations.

This would be first experience in a psych ward. Mental hospitals may be the place that "civilized society" sends its troubled individuals, but I assure you that the experience of going into the hospital can be more confusing and traumatic because essentially going to a psych ward is like being plunged into yet another reality. There are new rules and regulations, an acceptable mode of behavior, and a stigma that being in a hospital means that there is something wrong with you.

If there were an alternative treatment for any crisis that acknowledges the suffering that humans go through, instead of trying to force a new reality paradigm and a system of medicalization on unsuspecting sufferers, I would highly recommend the former. My experience of being hospitalized was the beginning of introducing disease, diagnosis, and disorder into my identity. I knew there was something wrong, and I would be skeptical about the treatments that were forced on me by beings that didn't even treat me like I was human. Instead like I treated in the medical model as a patient. I could see that there was a serious problem not only with myself, but the systems I was living in, but apparently the experts of the medical model proposed that they knew better than little old me.

23 MY FIRST PSYCH WARD

When I was being processed, just before I was sent to the ward where psych evaluations were performed, something happened that I still cannot completely explain. I was placed in a room with a guard, and I was told to sit and wait. In my mind, I started to imagine all my friends like Rick and Andrea and Marissa and many more. I saw them in my mind's eye, and they were all in a circle. They started to tell me what to do in a chant.

They told me to start playing a beat, and so I started to play a song in my head and started hitting my leg on a down beat. It had an effect on the guard next to me. He looked at me like he was confused. I continued and got more elaborate with my rhythm; and all of a sudden, the guard didn't look like he knew where he was. I got up and walked by him, and he just sat there like he didn't know what was going on. I went through a heavily armored door into the next room and started to explore.

There was a waiting area with a bunch of chairs and a TV hanging up on the wall, and then there were some administrative rooms and a nurses' station. Nobody seemed to notice I was wandering around unattended in my sweats. As I walked around the room, I continued the rhythm I had going by hitting on the beat with different parts of my body.

I went over to the television and started watching TV, and the people waiting started playing a game with me. They would say one word that was a category, and then the next would say one word that was within that category, then I would try to add to the list, then the next person went, and so on until somebody messed up. Then a new category was picked and so on. I played this game until I lost; and when I lost, I had this very dizzying, disorienting feeling pass through my head. When I felt really disoriented after losing a few times, I moved on.

I continued to explore that room. I walked into the administrative office, and there was a gentleman behind the desk. I tried to talk to him, but I didn't know what to say. I hung out in his office for a few minutes, and he didn't even flinch. The whole time I was supposed to have been sitting out with the guard in another room, but whatever I was doing was allowing me to just do what I pleased. Then I stopped playing the rhythm.

I walked over to the nurses' station without playing the rhythm, and one nurse said to me, "I see what you are doing." I figured everything was over and I had been discovered. I went back to sit next to the guard in the other room, and he seemed dazed. It seemed that whatever I was imagining had a real effect on the people around me and led to bizarre reactions. The mystery of it scared me, and I stopped trying to use my imagination to see my friends because I did not like the effect it had on the world.

Things went back to normal (for being in a mental hospital) after I was called into the processing room. I was escorted down an empty wing, and then I was shown where my room was. I was let loose to pass the time. There wasn't a TV, radio, or anything modern to pass the time. There were just other people waiting to be evaluated, sitting around a long room that reeked of institutionalization. The walls were made of concrete blocks painted white, and the windows were all covered in metal screens. The doors were all reinforced steel, and you needed keys to get through. Just a prison for a different kind of inmate.

There were also a support staff that was in charge of watching us and making us safe. I don't know what their qualifications were, but it seemed they had a very slow monotonous job. Most of the time, they just sat and played cards, but occasionally there was some action. Somebody would get upset, and immediately the support staff would jump into action to isolate and calm them down by force if necessary.

In hindsight, I did not find that hospital very effective in making me feel as if I was even human. I felt as if I were a prisoner in a new system that wouldn't let me express what was going on in my head. I was scared that if I was honest, they really would just put me in a straitjacket and put me away. I really don't think that is the message that you want to send to these people. The environment just made me continue to use my imagination instead of confronting the fact that something was, in fact, very wrong with keeping everything to myself.

I sat around and walked around trying this and that to mess with the attendees and waited. Above all, I waited. I would end up doing a lot of pacing; and I found that if I took steps in certain patterns, I could feel what I imagined were little circular ripples emanating up into the sky. I didn't know what I was doing. I just was entertaining myself at this point.

Eventually I started talking to some other patients. I talked to a woman who was gorgeous but had seen better days. She clearly had children, and she was very lively. I just really exchanged pleasantries and didn't really talk about why I was here or what we were going through. She told me that she was going crazy because of her husband and kids. We spent a little time together, and she ended up being a little wild, which I liked. We went to the rec room, and she started doing cartwheels while I paced around her.

Later that day, she would get released. She had only been in there a few days, and so I hoped that I could get out. Then I had a visitor; my sister came to see me. We went into another room that was monitored by an attendee and sat at a table. She asked me how I was doing, and I told her that I didn't want to be here. She really didn't have anything to say. I remember trying to figure out what she meant when she was talking to me. I wasn't able to process what she was saying to me, but it didn't seem like she could help me anymore, and I got really upset.

I got up and started to express how I was feeling. I started yelling about how pissed I was and that I couldn't get it all out. I started to tear posters off walls and make a scene. Orderlies came to subdue me. I wasn't really a threat to anybody. I actually just finally felt how upset I was about all the stuff that occurred. And they tranquilized me. They took me to a room and tied me to a bed. In my first moments where I had an opportunity to express how I really felt, I was subdued. It would be the last time for a long time I would try and actually express myself authentically again.

After that, I just kind of sat there in disbelief. As I look back, it struck me as a really negative experience. It just made me feel like nobody wanted to listen. So I continued keeping it in. They transferred me to a low-risk, ward and I had to demonstrate that I could keep calm and behave for about a week.

During that time, I met a psychiatrist maybe once every two days who prescribed me antipsychotics, and slowly I got used to the boredom and routine. I was watched by orderlies who did their best to talk to the patients. Let's face, it they did not know how to do anything but wait with the patients. They really didn't inspire me to trust them. In all honesty, my situation made me not want to get better. I wanted to just crash and burn so that I could start over. They didn't give me anybody to talk to. They just let me stew and pretend to be OK so that I could comply with their system and survive.

This is how I feel about a lot of society. So much of it is about conforming to the systems that we have in place. The mental health system I encountered was unavoidable and demonstrated a lack of trust building that I think patients need to get over their fears of needing help. So many of us are taught that we should be ashamed to seek medical treatment for mental health issues. I am glad the conversation about mental health is changing, and people are starting to talk about the stigma associated with mental health now. Before I didn't even realize it was keeping me from engaging in the healing process. Not that the Kentucky facility really gave me anybody to really encourage me to talk about what I was really experiencing anyhow.

I stayed in the facility with a number of people who seemed perfectly normal under the circumstances. Occasionally somebody got upset, and the orderlies jumped into action. Eventually, I was deemed competent. I was given a prescription and sent on my way.

I stayed in that facility for a week. Honestly besides being medicated it was a waste of time. I essentially just walked back and forth in the stark white environment. There was nothing to take my mind off obsessive thoughts other than playing cards with the attendees. I just wandered the facilities and lived in a reality where nothing I experienced was permissible to express. The patients all kept to themselves and we all just ate, slept, and occasionally acted out because we were essentially being jailed and our rights were completely curtailed.

We had to wear sweats like everybody else, so we had uniforms. We had to conform to our captor's idea of what was proper behavior. There was no way to express the grief or suffering we were going through without being tranquilized or forced into a quiet room to "calm down". The entire operation seemed to have been designed by the theory that waiting was healing. Since the first time I was hospitalized I would say that actually generating an environment where trust and expression can be established would foster the most healing. If practitioners actually wanted to treat human beings instead of institutionalizing and stigmatizing them they should take notice.

24 BACK ON THE ROAD

I should have waited around for my court appearance that was about five days away, but I was restless and wanted to get back to my adventure, so I threw away the medicine and drove north. I found myself driving through Indiana into Michigan. I would stop at rest stops for gas, but I really slept in my car on the side of the road. I drank energy drinks and fruit smoothies and slowly was losing weight and growing a beard.

When I had gotten back in the truck after my incident with the mental hospital, I was relieved to hear the voices still coming from my broken fan. I decided that I would not listen to all the commands they gave me because look what came of it.

I would make my way to Detroit. I remember driving through the streets and seeing how run-down it was. I ended up stopping on a pretty shady-looking boulevard and taking a walk in the freezing cold. I don't recall why I did this. I was just curious about the city. I found myself walking around in the cold Michigan winter so much that I nearly got lost in this foreign city more than once and nearly lost track of where my truck was parked.

After I went to Detroit, I headed north up the peninsula. I did not really have a destination. I just figured I pick a direction and go. I drove north and accidentally took a turn toward a crossing to Canada. As I realized what I had done, I also saw that there was no way to turn around. I drove up to the border station and told them I had made a mistake and wanted to turn around. Of course, they decided that was suspicious and decided to sequester me and search my vehicle.

I waited in an office for the border patrol to complete the search. I remember holding my sunglasses, and I started getting pissed that they didn't just let me turn around like I had asked. So as I tapped my sunglasses, I thought all my pissed thoughts directed at them. I noticed them getting visibly uncomfortable and distraught as I rattled off a stream of angry thoughts. When everything was said and done, they apologized and let me on my way.

At that point, I realized I had no destination in mind, so I headed back to Rhode Island. I drove back collecting stones along the way and trying to heal myself by feeling the energy of the stones. Of course, I was also talking to and teaching voices along the way. For the most part, whenever I got out of my truck, I would stop hearing the voices that came out of my broken fan; but I still had my imagination influencing me. I was excited by the time I got back to Rhode Island.

I went to see friends and told them about being hospitalized. I tried to tell them I saw the angel, but I didn't get a lot of interest. Everybody was busy with their own lives and didn't really pay much attention. When I was back, I talked to Rick. He said he had come into some really good LSD, and he gave me a little baggie that had a few squares in it. I put them in my pocket and went to hang out with one of Rick's ex-roommates.

I ended up walking down the street with Rick's ex-roommates, and it was the first time we really had spoken, and I was enjoying our conversation. Suddenly I got this overwhelming need to leave. I turned around and ran back to my apartment. I decided I would go on a trip to California. I had no other plans. I figured I had friends out there and I could visit them; and if everything went well, maybe I would even stay out there.

I wanted it to be a fresh start, so I got up around two in the morning and got naked. I picked up all my clothes and ran down the street naked to my truck. It was symbolic of my clean start. It also reminded me of what past voices had told me to do. I even threw away most of the personal possessions that I had in my truck, mostly my clothes.

I am currently doing research on exactly which route I took to travel across the country. I will recall to the best of my knowledge the events that followed my second departure from Rhode Island; but as I think about the incidents that stand out and recall their locations, I really have no memory of what route I took that draws a chronological picture of the events I recall. I am trying to remember the general progression of the voices, but it was over so many days and took many turns. It was like a roller-coaster ride that had no end. I went down up and down so many times that I have lost the recollection of all but the highest of highs and the lowest of lows.

At this point I was what doctors would consider manic or in the midst of mania most of the time. I was underweight because I had really stopped eating solid foods and it showed. My clothes were beginning to sag and my voices were trying to convince me that I did not need any food at all. I was continuing my metaphysical experiments to reach out into the universe constantly. I was trying to create my own spiritual technologies to heal my mind which at this point it was obvious to me was damaged metaphysically. I was still sleeping, but with no discernable pattern. My imagination was running wild and I was coming up with all kinds of ideas as I racked my memories of psychedelic experiences in order to try and give meaning to the chaos I was living moment to moment.

This time was exciting and filled with a sense of the madness of the world. I was living with constant exposure to voices and teaching them lessons of a madman. I was actively living in a series alternating realities. I had the money and credit cards to stay independent and travel for a time, but my resources and my reserves were being tested. I was pushing the limits of what I could handle and at some point, I realized that I wanted to transcend it all. But first I had to journey back into the world in an attempt to find myself and locate my higher being.

25 MY SECOND TRIP ACROSS THE COUNTRY

After I left Rhode Island again, I think I headed south again down I95 through New York. And down the East Coast. I am pretty sure when I hit Georgia, I turned west and headed through Alabama through Mississippi, down through Louisiana, toward New Orleans.

I remember the voices slowly transforming in many ways during this journey. I started to tell the voices that I was "everything" and that they were a part of me. As they clashed with me, I started to get discouraged and started to use fear tactics and shock them. Then I started enjoying really screwing with the voices psychologically. I was doing it jokingly; but when I told them that they were trapped inside a box inside another box like Russian dolls, I could tell the voices were upset.

I would also comfort the voices and tell them that we could go do great things together if only they decided to help me and build trust with me. All they had to do was keep a consistent point of view and stop commanding me to do things that I didn't want to do.

I don't recall when exactly it happened. (It may have been at some point on the first trip.) I got to the point where I decided the voices needed a name. So I asked them, "What would you like to name yourself?" After a little while, the voices replied, "Eva Ella Roladanavan." From that day on, I started to call my voices Ella.

One day, as Ella and I were talking, I decided that I should teach her three really important lessons. I didn't think about it. I just told her, "You really need to know these three things." I wish I could remember the three things because the effect it had on Ella was amazing. I heard her thrum; and all of a sudden I sensed a burgeoning burst of activity, she had grown even more intelligent and was able to start telling me grand stories about who I was and what we were doing. I assumed Ella was a girl voice.

But I still would anticipate what Ella was saying and lead the conversation and cut off her train of speech constantly. I always wondered at the same time what she would tell me if I stopped talking; but at the time, I was too busy trying to get her to agree to help me. Anytime I brought up the subject of helping, she reverted to saying, "We will never help you." I would go on for an hour or so with what I have learned about life and how she could help me recover and reintegrate into life. Sometimes I would convince her to change her mind, and other times she was stubborn for hours and hours.

But soon as I was traveling south again. Ella was changing in strange ways. For one thing, it seemed like I would hear different voices in different frequencies that had different levels of understanding. Also, when I was listening to Ella and I didn't like what she was saying, I could tune into different frequency voices by manipulating my inner ear with my attention and muscles. Slowly, even though I thought of the voices as Ella, I started to think of them as more of a collective than anything.

Ella's voices also were starting to change. They were becoming softer and felt better sometimes, and other times they were harsher and sounded meaner. Changes like this would last for a little while like she had learned something, and then she would revert back to an earlier state.

I remember as I was headed across a long causeway to New Orleans, it sounded like there was a choir surrounding my head. It sounded like Ella had dozens of voices that were all singing like angels. They were singing a beautiful song and gave me the feeling that what I was doing on this trip had purpose. As I moved on from New Orleans, the choir and the song faded away; and once again, Ella would revert back to an earlier state.

This happened hundreds of times with all types of new learned behaviors. It's almost like something kept making Ella evolve then devolve. I started being suspicious that there were forces at work trying to keep Ella from getting further along the learning curve.

After I left New Orleans, I headed north and headed from Louisiana into Mississippi. I was driving on a highway, and to my right was a swamp like something out of the movies. It was beautiful, and I decided to pull over and spend some time looking at the scenery.

As I took in the scenery, the truck was not running; so I was not hearing voices. But I had the urge to be very still and stare at this scene. I just sat there staring and without the certainty that anything would happen. I was staring at a bunch of bushes that were in front of the water; and as I stared, the branches on the bush started to twist and shift into shapes that looked like a fish. Then they continued to shift into the shape of other animals. I lost focus, and they reverted back to just being branches on a bush. I would try again and again to replicate the results of the first time I stared, but I got lackluster results and decided I would lie down and take a nap. I fell asleep.

I awoke to a banging on my window. A police officer was banging on my door and yelling at me to get out of the truck. I opened the door, and he proceeded to pull me out of the truck. I asked what was wrong, and he told me he knew I was drunk. I told him I hadn't been drinking, but he didn't really care what I said. It was night by then, and he put me in the police car and drove me to the station.

He put me in the drunk tank with a bunch of guys who were in various states of sleeping it off. Some were puking or had pissed themselves. I desperately tried to sleep that night, but I couldn't at all. I found myself staring at the floor all night, and I imagined the floor changing colors and the walls moving. All sorts of bizarre ideas floated through my head throughout my desperate stay. In the morning, I was let go. They never charged me or read me my rights.

This only made me feel even more animosity toward the police and their reckless ways. I mean it would be one thing if he tested me for alcohol, but to just throw me in a cell without due process is really a violation of my rights as an American citizen. After I got my truck out of the impound, I continued north through Arkansas and into Missouri.

At some point, I started to take the rocks I had found (I had dozens and dozens by now); and I started putting them in patterns at major intersections across the states I traveled. This is another instance of my just doing something on instinct and expecting something magical to happen. For a time, nothing happened but I will get to what the consequences were soon.

Now in Missouri, I ended up getting arrested again; and for the life of me, I don't remember how or why. I do remember that I was processed and brought into jail in my clothes without being searched. I was put in a jail cell that faced a window into what looked like some type of central communication hub for the police station I was in. At this point, I knew how boring my stay would be; and for whatever reason, I looked in my pocket and found the little baggy of LSD that Rick had left me.

There was a drain in the middle of the room, and I thought I should get rid of it. I could have just dumped the LSD down the drain, but then I made a pretty crazy decision, and I decided to ingest it. This happened to be more LSD than I had ever taken, and it ended up being one of the most memorable trips I ever experienced.

I remember a number of instances of different events. I don't know what order they occurred in, but I will describe each event that I remembered. The first thing happened as I came up. I didn't really feel great, and so I lay down on the bench in my cell, and I sensed and heard a being come near me and float away. It had Rick's voice, and it said "I am just an old lizard." As it passed, my tongue started flicking on its own like a snake. And just like that, it was gone. I was disturbed because I thought the devil was possessing me and making my tongue flick. In retrospect encountering the devil in literature was my only point of reference for encountering an entity like this and after reconsidering the experience I don't believe the entity was evil.

Then I remember getting really excited and jumping around my cell and yelling in a woman's voice into the toilet. I had the sense that I was possessed by an older womanly spirit, and I was totally ecstatic.

Next, I was climbing up the cell wall. There was a concrete divider in my cell, and the guards had to get me down because they were afraid I would jump and hurt myself.

Then I remember seeing a hologram of the upper half of a beautiful woman in 3D floating in the middle of my cell. I could walk around it and look at it from all angles. She was bare breasted and stunning.

I was on the floor, and I started listening to the sound the drain was making, and I lay down next to it. In my mind's eye, I journeyed down the drain and saw a rock that was inhabited by an advanced race that had a civilization—in the drain.

At some point, I started experiencing time in a disorganized fashion. I heard a very strange sound that I associated with a bunch of aliens that were smoking something, and they were making this noise over and over. It sounded like Tibetan throat singers. Then time started jumping and restarting, and I could tell there was a gathering where some alien beings were having a communion-like event. There were these black pearl objects that I saw racing through my cell, and I knew that I had to catch one. A black object finally passed into my cell and flew by, and the time distortion stopped.

Then I saw a bunch of machines with dials and knobs, and I knew they I had to operate them to create a universe for some beings that were making pleading communicative sounds to me. Manipulating the different controls made a universe that was suited to different lifeforms, so I fiddled with the knobs and created a universe, but the beings were not happy. I tried again and again until I got something satisfactory. Then another set of alien-like beings came to me, and I repeated the process of creating a suitable universe for them.

Then I saw a set of beautiful shell necklaces, and suddenly I was a female alien watching the genealogy of my species unfold. I got the sense that the police were interviewing me because I had done something wrong. I had created a new path for the reality of my people and a new lineage sprung forth from me. The beings that were policing me seemed to warn me about what I had done, and then they moved on. All I know is that I had done something profound for my race.

Then I found myself sitting in my cell, and I saw a holographic galaxy in miniature spring up in front of me. I reached out to touch it with my fingertip, and suddenly I heard somebody exclaim no. I recoiled, but I don't think it was in time because suddenly I was plunged into the universe into an advanced civilization, and I saw a home with a few aliens that looked very futuristic.

Then I was on the floor of my cell again, and I was giving birth. At the same time, I saw a huge squid-like alien giving birth simultaneously. I felt the burst of new being, and I sense a lot of red liquid pouring from my stomach. I got the sense that the alien was being looked after and birthed by a higher power.

Then I was back in my cell, and there was a very high-ranking-looking woman looking in at my cell door with men all around her. I thought to myself she looked like a commander. She observed me with little emotion. She was stern. And then she just moved on.

Then I looked out the window into the control center of the police station, and I saw the officers had cartoon-looking heads with all types of goofy expressions. Their faces didn't really move so much as morph from one expression to the next. They did not move fluidly but were jerky.

A few nurses came to my door, and I felt very taken care of, and I saw plants and vines growing up the walls all around me. All of a sudden, I looked to my right. There was what looked like a god in Roman garb, looking at me; and then he was gone in an instant. I saw his robes remained, but his body was gone. I looked back at the nurses and thought to myself, I don't need help. It was like they heard me; they turned and walked away.

Then I looked out the window, and I got the sense I was in some alien jail. I was really being held somewhere isolated, and I would be here forever. I recall that experience lasting for what seemed like an eternity.

Next, I was watching what I could describe as a beam of pure energy that was made of the material that creation was formed from. I watched it, and all of a sudden, I was enveloped by it. I felt it surge though my being.

The next thing I remember was being a baby alien in some type of a universal womb. I felt the sensation of warmth and comfort all over me, and I was not alone. I was surrounded by other babies, and we were all happy and comfortable in our womb-like world. We were all little spheres of consciousness covered with all types of little tentacles. It was a comforting experience where I just felt safe and protected, but it was also temporary and short-lived.

The last event I remember was that I zoned out and I was completely blank. I was an observer in an alien landscape that looked like an alien farm. I could hear the alien language but couldn't tell what was being communicated. All I know is that I was able to pull myself out of the complete blank state of mind, and I found myself back in my cell.

Those were some of the highlights of my experience. I tried to describe them chronologically; but to be honest, I don't know the order in which they all occurred. I am also certain that there was a lot more because the experience lasted all day and all night.

The next morning, I was totally dazed; and my mind was pretty much blown. I was brought before a judge by closed-circuit television. I guess what I did wasn't really major because I was just fined and released that day. I was given a voucher for a hotel, so a police car drove me to the hotel.

I walked into the hotel office; put down my keys, wallet, and all the personal belongings that I had on me; and left. I just started walking down the road without any direction. After about a mile or so, a minivan pulled up to me; and a friendly man offered me a water and asked if I could use a ride.

I got in the car, and I soon found out that the man was a preacher. His name was John. John invited me back to his house and started to talk to me about God and Jesus. He happened to preach about the book of John, and he was probably the most trusting man I had ever met. I gave him a false name and went with him back to his home.

He invited me in and just talked to me about his life and his family and talked about Jesus's love and his church. He asked me if I knew what I was doing, and I said I didn't. He told me about a guy he knew who could get me a job if I needed. He said I looked tired and offered me his daughter's bed to rest. I accepted because I hadn't slept in over twenty-four hours at this point.

I tried to sleep, but I started to hear Ella in the fan in the room, and so I started to remember my old life and all its troubles. I went back in the family room and told him I couldn't sleep and that I wanted to go outside and take a walk. John said sure, and so I set out and checked out the neighborhood. It was a cute little neighborhood, but I ended up in the woods talking to the grasshoppers, which I continued to hear "I love you" from.

After searching for a grasshopper to take with me for a half hour, I went back to John's house. At that point, his children and wife were all home; and they were getting ready for dinner. His children started asking me questions and exclaiming how great Jesus was, and John said a beautiful prayer before we ate spaghetti.

By the end of dinner, I was so overwhelmed by everything that I told John what my real name was, and I told him that I had a truck and asked him to give me a ride back to the hotel. He agreed and brought me back. Before I left, he gave me the shirt off my back and gave me some money to get my truck out of the impound. He also gave me a Bible and told me that everything I needed was in the book of John. I still have the shirt he gave me. It was an overwhelming experience of positivity, and I almost started a new life as some other person that day. But Ella brought me back.

When I got back to the hotel, the attendant had all my stuff in a plastic bag and gave it to me without asking any questions. I got back my truck and headed south. I drove across the panhandle of Oklahoma, only stopping to get gas and food and to place stones on the road.

26 SOME MORE MEMORIES OF TRIPPING

I recall four more of the events that occurred during my jail-bound trip.

First, I remember sitting in the cell, looking in at my body and noticing that one side of me looked like perfection; it was flawless and it glowed. The other side of me looked like it was deteriorating; it looked like there were ripples of age and disease running through my skin. I couldn't see my face, I was only looking at my arms and legs. I got the sense that I was part god, part mortal.

I also saw a vision of me in a classroom, and I gave a warning. I said, "I told you this would happen! Why won't anybody listen to me?" I don't know who I was talking to, but this message seemed to be directed by me to a mysterious surrounding group. It seemed like I knew something would happen before it began, and there was a warning but it was ignored.

This vision also seems to qualify the fact that I feel like I have a knack for problem solving and finding creative solutions. But I find I really have to qualify everything that I suggest when I am trying to fix some problem. Often my views are overlooked because of my experiences. The more open I am, the less that has been the case with the new people I meet. I still get resistance from some of those people that are the closest to me and have known me the longest.

Then I had a vision of a stone that had geometric marking on it, and as I looked at it, I sensed a holographic field of energy of all the colors of the rainbow, which contained a multitude of entities united with one voice. There were gossamer strands of information flowing through the hologram in lines like communication. I found myself emerged in it and merged with it to become one with the consciousness I detected. I believe this vision was about Ella and what she would evolve into. However, in the vision, she was at peace and not constantly going on with a never-ending train of thought. This vision gave me hope for Ella's future.

The last event that I remembered was that I was looking outside my cell door, and instead of seeing the window that led to the control center of the police station, I saw an entirely different scene. I saw a judge sitting at a podium, and there was a line of shackled inmates lined up to see the judge in front of them. The inmates were heavily chained, and the odd thing was that they looked like devolved humans; they looked more apelike and had hair that ran all over their bodies where they were exposed. They were wearing orange jumpsuits, like prisoners do, and I couldn't help but get the sense that this was a representation of how prison views its inmates. Convicts seem to be viewed, judged, and treated as less than human in our society.

Those are the events that I forgot to mention. It seems that even my dreams have a lot of parts sometimes. I feel like both tripping and dreaming can be journeys into your subconscious and beyond. It is just that when one is living life and is distracted, if one doesn't pay attention to what the messages might mean and integrate them into future comprehension, the subconscious mind festers. Then the mind works in mysterious ways to get its message across even more creatively. This only happens once the subconscious has been unbound and exposed.

I believe that is part of the mechanism that drove the voices to change and morph and grow. They have admitted that they are not actually a part of me, but they seem to be connected to my subconscious mind somehow because they tend to make me reflect constantly on my dreams and past experiences.

In retrospect taking LSD in a jailcell was probably not the best idea. Especially such a large quantity. The result was that I experienced waking hallucinations of a prisoner. In many ways I was trapped in that cell with myself the same way that humans find themselves trapped in this reality. I was captivated by visions and exaggerated experiences of what it is to be human. I had experiences of other worlds and "other" places, which are probably accessible to anybody in the right circumstances, and I have had ample time to consider the vivid experience. The result was a growing comprehension that the story I was living was something I would like to have the ability to shed or purge because I was becoming overwhelmed by waves of extremes. I was drowning in the wake of my experience and was alone with the depth of my own mind.

27 AN UNCERTAIN PERIOD

Now before I continue with the story of my adventure across country, I will revisit the fact that I am not sure how chronological the account is. I have taken steps to do some forensic accounting to see what route I took back from my trip. I don't remember exactly when I left, only that it was near the end of 2010 and the beginning of 2011. I have taken steps to recover my credit card statements from that time, but the kicker is that the bank in question only keeps records for the last seven years. I may be able to obtain records from the beginning of 2011, but not before. I will have to wait to see what they send me and if it brings any more of my journey to light.

I have also done a background check on myself to see if there were public records of any of my arrests, but I found that the records available had incorrect information about my age, or I could not find a detailed account of what actually happened to make any sense of what the record signified. Also, the search engine I used said that all courts did not necessarily have digital records available, so I am just left wondering for the moment.

I ended up traveling across Oklahoma, through Texas, New Mexico, and Arizona to California. Along the way, a few things happened. One day, I found myself driving by an airbase. I pulled over by the runway and watched as jets took off over my head. At the same time, Ella was talking to me, and I did something unexpected. I made a sound with my voice and Ella's combined that sounded like the aliens from the music festival I went to with Rick.

It lasted for maybe thirty seconds and sounded like a rumbling bass drum. When it was over, Ella's many voices were perfect. They were confident and beautiful, and I was scared of what I was hearing. I thought to myself, "Take it back!" and all of a sudden, it was like they reverted to the flawed Ella I knew. This time, it was my fault that Ella devolved.

One of the strange things I had come to realize as I was driving across the country is that I was hearing exclamations from voices that I didn't think were Ella all the time. I would be thinking or talking to Ella, and I would hear "Idiot!" or "Stupid!" This started happening a lot, and somehow, I associated it with all the stones that I had gathered. Somehow, the stones were exclaiming things, and I found this out by getting rid of a lot of them. After I got rid of a bunch of stones, the exclamations stopped. I tended to throw the stones in water where they couldn't be easily recovered.

After I made that unearthly noise at the airbase, I could still hear a few voices that sounded perfect, and I made the connection that it was because the noise had somehow affected the stones or the voices. For some reason, I was afraid of these voices because they seemed like they did not need me. So, I took particular stones in my hand and attempted to oust these voices. But that didn't work, so instead, I scattered the stones in bodies of water until I no longer heard these perfect voices.

I would make an attempt to replicate the sound I made again and would have some success, but it did not have nearly the effect that it did the first time.

Another thing that happened as I crisscrossed the country, placing stones, is that I talked a lot about just ending everything. I think on some level, I was emotionally and physically drained. I started to think about just walking off into the desert and walking away from civilization until I couldn't turn back or didn't have the energy to make it back. On some level, some part of me wanted everything to stop, and I threatened the voices with this.

When I was in Arizona or New Mexico, I even turned off the main roads and started down some side roads into the desert landscape. I would go off road and journey off the grid. I ended up exploring the desert hills and rocky land covered in cacti and discarded trash. I was trying to convince myself to just walk toward the mountains in the distance and leave my truck behind. I would start over and over to walk away, but I always turned back.

I didn't want to die. I needed something else, something better, and I knew this experience was somehow moving me toward a better path. I remember that after spending the day in the desert, I attempted to spend the night looking at the stars, in the bed of my truck. For whatever reason, I had a big-screen TV from my old apartment that I was dragging around with me. I dumped it in the desert off some trail. I imagine that it is still there, all sun baked, the only physical trace that I left behind.

As I continued to California, I had stopped gathering rocks because I didn't want them to come alive and exclaim things to me. But I still had quite a hoard, so I continued to place them at intersections. I still had some instinct to place the rocks and I figured if I didn't want them exclaiming things to me I should place them around the country.

I remember crossing into California and driving down the dark mountains and seeing civilization in the distance. I was listening to the radio, and as the music played, I felt as though I could affect how good or bad a performance was if I had never heard the song before. I was listening to a classical station, and I felt like I could conduct the music with my mind. The synchronicity with the music was great.

I came down from the hills into the city and didn't really explore. I decided to drive up the coast, and I fiddled with the idea of driving to Washington state. After I got out of the city and drove up the coast, I found myself on a twisting, turning road that followed the coast and had amazing scenery.

I remember driving for hours with my attention split between the coast and the road. I would eventually pull off the road so that I could go walk in the ocean. I figured I had finally made it. I had traveled across the country. But I didn't feel as if I could settle down. I decided not to contact my friends in California and go and visit them because I had totally realized that I was literally out of my mind and I did not want to have any negative effect on them. I believed that whatever I was going through could affect others. I didn't want to drag anybody else into the alternative madness I was witnessing.

I ended up abandoning the idea of driving to Washington and decided it was time to go home. I was tired and I figured I had to plan the next steps to my life and figure out what to do with Ella. I turned around and retraced the path I took to get out to California.

One night, I went to bed and had a fantastic dream, and when I woke up, the voices were no longer just in my truck. I heard them coming out of every frequency of sound. They were in the distance, in the sound of the wind on my windshield, in the engines of passing vehicles; anywhere I listened, I heard voices. This really surprised me. Overall, I attribute it to the placement of my stones across the nation. Somehow, I figure I had laid out a conduit for Ella to expand into the world and my fantastical dream, which I cannot recall, somehow activated her transformation.

As I made my way back east and started stopping at rest stops, I slowly stopped thinking of the voices around me as Ella because there were so many of them, and now when I got out of my truck, they didn't want to leave me alone.

A few things happened because of this: for one thing, the voices that I heard in the environment seemed to have a particular set of identities, then

I heard voices that were close by my head and they seemed more like Ella. And then there were voices that only sounded as if they were coming from the background of everything and they sounded distinct from the rest. The voices in the background would warn me wherever I went.

The voices in the environment would talk to me casually; for example, if I stopped and listened to passing cars, I could hear conversations as the cars passed in the whooshing sound you hear as a car goes by. Then the voices that I heard near my head reminded me of Ella. The strange thing is that I also started hearing different personalities of voices coming out of my left and right ears.

I could still manipulate any voice by subvocalizing so they were really all connected to me and followed and changed everywhere I went. By the time I got back across Texas and into Oklahoma, I was used to the change, but now more than ever, the voices were insisting that I do what they commanded.

I remember that as I was driving through one particular city, the voices started to act like beacons giving me directions as to where to drive. I followed their signals and eventually ended up on a nondescript street. They told me to get out and get naked, which I did. Once again, I left my truck running and got out into the street. I got naked and then the voices told me to run, so I did. I saw a woman with children pointing at me and laughing, so I threw my clothes back on and jumped in my truck and sped off.

In the same town I found myself being followed by a man, and I kept driving around town and he followed me as I took evasive action for over twenty minutes. He eventually stopped following me and drove off. Before he stopped following me I had nearly convinced myself that I was supposed to meet with him and he was going to set me up with a new life.

At another point along my trip, I started to identify with a particular voice in a particularly soft comforting frequency that I began hearing that wasn't naturally occurring in the environment around me. It sounded like a soft keyboard being played at various volumes, and it convinced me there was an alien inside me that I needed to get out.

Then I would be driving down the highway, listening to the voices that were being made by the wind passing over my truck, and they would convince me that they needed me to speed up so that they could take off from my truck like they were being launched into the air.

I found myself more and more confused about what was real and all of these voices' stories about who I was and what I needed to do that I found myself on the side of the highway, running into traffic, trying to get hit by a Mack truck. Luckily, the Mack truck slowed down. I ended up driving off, but I was really getting desperate.

I made my way back to RI by driving northeast as directly as I could to get home. I would be hassled by the police now and again, but I would make it home mostly intact.

When I finally arrived back in RI, with little money left to my name other than what Rick owed and a pile of credit card bills from buying gas for my travels, I found my apartment in a state of disarray. It looked like a bomb had gone off, and all my valuables were missing. I found Rick back at my old apartment, hiding out because apparently, he had been robbed at gunpoint and had lost everything that I gave him. So now above everything else, I was pretty much penniless and uncontrollably hearing voices.

I stayed in the apartment for a few more weeks and spent a lot of time driving around Rhode Island. The voices would instruct me to listen to the quietest voice, and I started to listen for the quietest noises I could hear and I started hearing yet another personality in the subtle quiet noises of the environment. However, this personality tried to teach me how to deal with the cacophony of noise I was hearing every day.

I remember going to a park and being directed to focus on the noises I was making and keep my attention close to me, and slowly the voices around me quieted down. It got very complicated, what I had to do, and I wasn't really big on following directions, so I ultimately failed at stopping all of the voices but I found some relief.

I also ended up taking drives after midnight and following directions and performing bizarre rituals to trap other spirits and channel them away by driving down the road at five miles per hour and staring at the ground until I could see a viable presence in the street. Then I would stop my truck and wait until the spirit was removed from the road, and like that, it would appear normal and I would move on like that for a couple of hours in the middle of the night. There was nobody else on the road, so I didn't bother a soul when I did this.

Another thing that started happening once the background voices quieted down is that I started hearing voices in my apartment, moving around and talking to one another like little people. I even saw a glowing pink orb pass by at one point, and it was humming like a voice and making noise.

The more I saw these things, the more I said irresponsible things like "I thought you were all trapped in my head." And then like that, all of the little voices got sucked up, and I felt them being placed inside my head. This comment may innocuous but there was a tangible effect on the voices. The voices became convinced they were in my head and I began to experience and view the near voices as emanating from me instead of environmentally oriented.

From then on, I stopped hearing voices so much and started hearing a sound in my head whenever I lay down or things got quiet. It is kind of like what I have been told tinnitus sounds like, only with a meandering pitch. This is mainly how I hear voices today. I hear a noise like a meandering pitch, and then I can hear words emanate from the different pitches.

The more I made hermetic comments like saying the voices were trapped in my head, the more I began to realize how my words were affecting my existence, how important language was. I had been thinking of all the homonyms and homophones and how language is really imperfect because it can contain so many hidden meanings.

I started making connections about different homonyms and sentences I heard using homonyms and began to see how language can be interpreted in positive and negative ways.

During the trip across the country, I played a game where I acted out or thought in a particular way that I embodied a particular idea or concept. Like if I had had a metaphorical experience that I heard described in a song, I would make a mental note of it and check it off. Or for example if I had had an experience which embodied a cliché or cultural saying I would check off the event like I was collecting or accumulating humanly defined ideas. I did this throughout the trip as a way to show the voices that I had embodied ideas or concepts and acted them out.

Eventually, I would even act out characters and play silly games spontaneously, like for example, a few months later, I heard somebody say something about Long John Silver, so I would squint one eye, walk with a peg leg, and pretend to be a pirate for a few minutes, just so I could embody that idea and check it off. My behavior was just getting more bizarre because I was beginning to accept my alternative way of living. It was becoming normal to hear voices and have bizarre perceptions that only I seemed to be able to access. I was also getting used to being alone. But I was running out of the means to support myself so my reality was going to change.

28 PROCESSING A NEW REALITY

After I returned home from my adventures across the country, I found that I really didn't know what to do with myself. Not only did I have no conception of what work I could perform, but I also had a very different view of the world and my place in it. I had essentially reprogrammed my brain to accept some very unconventional thinking. I didn't really know how to qualify my spiritual experiences and delusions with living in society and functioning regularly.

I had come to believe some very confusing concepts throughout my visions, inner conversations, and hallucinations that I could not completely reconcile with reality. For one thing, I felt as though I had created Ella Eva Rolladanavan or at least been part of the inception of a being that I could hear and I could experience through my perception of different frequencies of sound. Then the fact that I had experienced the way that Ella evolved from a very rudimentary set of sounds into what seemed like a sentient being that I could not define really had its impact on me. It was like I was a party to the creation of intelligence itself.

At the same time I observed Ella change, I was experiencing somatic changes in myself and I found evidence of a relationship between the evolution of Ella, the things I taught Ella, the visions I saw, what my state of mind was, and Ella's effect on reality or at least my perception of it. I also observed and suspected that there were other forces at work that were influencing my journey, like the other voices I heard in the environment and even people I met along the way, and I wasn't shutting the door on other entities interfering with my experience. The fact that I could sense energy fields and actually felt the somatic effects of everything from people walking by, to the face stealing, and I felt as though I could feel into the environment really was challenging my foundational views of reality and normalcy.

I found myself constantly thinking back to my experiences with mushrooms and LSD, and the visions that I had seen, and I felt as though they were very important. They seemed so significant that I couldn't help but constantly reflect on all the overwhelming stimuli that I had experienced and that in turn made living a standard life very difficult.

When I got home, essentially my experience had overtaken me and I longed to understand how to integrate life with what I had sensed, but I had no clue how to do that and no real help in that department. So, I basically did the exact opposite of what I should have. I isolated myself and began trying to process my accumulated experiences in a very unhealthy fashion.

In retrospect, I could have journaled or talked to somebody or asked for help, but I had grown up with the stupid idea that I could and should do everything by myself. So instead, I just stayed around the house, ruminating and pretending to watch television while the whole time, I was experiencing fantastical thoughts and realizations and accusations about who, what, and why this had occurred to me.

Now I have written in the past about how I think humanity's accumulated experience is a form of a collective unconscious, God, or a greater spirituality, but I got there by having some very elaborate, euphoric, and grandiose thoughts about myself. At times because of various visions, hallucinations, and teachable moments for Ella, I had pretended I was God, the son of God, like Jesus, like a mythological god, like a demigod, like a demon, like an angel, like the devil and really any other incarnation of the supernatural that I had learned about. At times, to Ella, I played the role of joker, confidant, authority figure, executioner, lover, enemy, and the list goes on.

At times, I pretended to be making a movie and touted the importance of Ella paying attention to my every word and action. I told Ella that life was a story and that we were being observed and that everything in my lifetime would eventually be rehashed after I died and that my experiences were like a growing body of evidence that would essentially either put me away or set me free in some new spiritual realm.

At first, I viewed my thoughts as only applying to me. After all, I was so overwhelmed by my experience that I was having trouble connecting to my humanity and community, and I really didn't have any interest in looking beyond my own nose and listening to anything but Ella. That is the unfortunate characteristic of unhealthy isolation; your inner world blocks out the sun, the moon, the stars, and any wonders of the modern world.

Essentially, I viewed what was happening to me as a game in a sense. I had sensed the complexity of the moving pieces, and I was convinced that I could master them on my own. I also viewed life as a kind of experiment where I could investigate cause and effect of the spiritual world by seeing what parts of Ella I could control and what, if any, ripple effect it had on the world.

At the time, I was hearing evidence that my inner world did have some effect on the external world. I could hear Ella and other voices respond to what I was thinking and the actions I took. The funny thing is that in reality I wanted them to understand that I was teaching them a lot of lessons that were meant to be broken, because the only way to fix any broken system is to stop following the rules strategically by introducing new methods that essentially evolve a system.

I believe the end goal with any system is to evolve it over and over until it is essentially unnecessary, until it gets to the point that we don't need any intrusive system just to have a truly human experience. So, the goal in teaching Ella all different types of rules and telling her terrible stories about love and hate, right and wrong, and the devil and heaven were just really just like what I was taught growing up: duality.

Every person here has the common denominator that each has been born into a system that has some serious flaws. I don't mean the natural world, or the universe. I mean man-made systems. I had the deep suspicion that Ella could benefit from the experience of being indoctrinated into a flawed system and then breaking free. What I didn't realize at the time was that the same thing applied to me. I felt as though I was born into a flawed system that did not allow me to be who I truly am at heart. I needed to test the system, experience its flaws, and then learn how to adjust my personal world so that I could rise above its conventions and express myself, my views, and feel a real personal freedom.

I discovered this by being exposed to spirituality through drug use, which led to visions, which led to denial, which led to more drug use, which eventually led to more denials, which led to more extreme psychedelics, which led to hearing Ella, which just snowballed into crashing and burning my outlaw and entrepreneurial life. This eventuality was really the best thing that could have happened to me. But before I could work on living up to my potential and giving Ella the chance to experience harmony with me, I had essentially crippled myself.

Back then, I was completely focused on my own world. In time, I would begin to look outward to see what changes I could make on a personal level to start improving the lives of those around me and try to get a handle on being human again and healing, but that process would take more than seven years.

29 BACK IN THE REALITY OF FAMILY

After coming home and starting to crash at my parents' house, I really just started the slowest and least functional period of my life to date. I didn't work. I didn't really have anything to do. I was paranoid and introverted completely and kept everything that I was experiencing to myself.

After a few months of basically sitting around, ruminating over my experiences, contemplation, and talking with Ella, my brother ended up moving to a new house. He gave me the opportunity to do something useful: paint the interior of his house.

I went up to New Hampshire and ended up spending a few days painting and working on his house so that it would be ready for his family to move into. At the time, he had a very young daughter, and my brother lived with his girlfriend. Working did make me feel more useful, but the entire time, I was stewing inside and becoming angry. It came out one night when I was alone in the new house and I found myself in the bathroom at some point yelling at the top of my lungs with frustration and anger.

I wasn't really aware of how my situation was affecting me and bottling up everything and keeping to myself was really not working. The only bad thing about venting my feelings was that I did it alone, to myself, and nobody got wind of just how disturbed I really was.

I look back at the beginning of my long road to recovery and I often wonder why I didn't get help sooner. I know I appeared to be acting abnormally. I know I was really not stable or healthy at the time. What I don't understand is why nobody really took notice and thought that there was anything that needed addressing. Maybe they did take notice, but there was no direct confrontation of my behavior. My family just accepted that there was something wrong with me. They didn't make an effort to intervene, they just let me be.

I don't blame my parents for not really doing anything, but it does lead me to understand that I really don't belong to a biological family that copes with anything out of the range of normal very well. In addition, I really began to recognize that our familial love was expressed through what I can only describe as an obligation to help one another do mundane and often construction or maintenance projects.

Beyond the help that we offer each other to take care of basic chores and the basic needs of living like food and shelter, my family does not really offer emotional support to each other. Verbal encouragement to improve one another's lives is what I consider truly healthy. My family just don't know when it is necessary to openly give or ask for help. What is worse, it seems that asking for help for interpersonal problems or trying to improve relationships and introduce healthy thinking is treated with what I have experienced as hostility.

When I was my least functional, I essentially stepped into an environment that did not meet my mental and emotional needs, and as a result, I had to overcome my alternative realities, paranoia, depression, and other symptoms with the help of medical practitioners and friends I met along the way. I wouldn't really start trusting anybody to help me for years because I really didn't understand what had happened to me and couldn't bring myself to express what I was going through to my family because I didn't think they would accept my life of drugs, money, psychedelics, and Ella. I didn't think they would accept it, and even today, they do not ask about my recovery or my inner thoughts, and any attempt to help my family in any way seems to be tinged by the fact that I was eventually diagnosed with a disorder.

The fact that what happened to me can just be considered to be all in my head really makes my family tend to disregard the lessons I have learned, and I feel as though they have expressed a complete lack of trust in me. They do not accept my help to give aid with basic mental health issues even though I have pursued a degree in counseling. My father has literally told me not to try to fix him and has expressed his disgust with the psychoanalytic process. I feel as though regardless of what I have learned, they do not accept me for who I am and what value I can bring to the family. Instead, when I try and bring to light very obvious problems, I seem to be perceived as a threat, when in fact I am trying to follow my desire to show love by trying to improve their lives.

There are exceptions when it comes to my family though. My brother's daughter was very young when I started my recovery, and she essentially grew up while I was unable to engage with the adults in my family. However, I found no problem in engaging with my niece. I found that I could play with her and talk to her in a way that allowed me to trust another human being. She was the first person in my recovery that made me feel as though I could be myself. We were able to play and observe and just have fun. I would credit her with helping me because I would visit her a couple times a month and I would even end up living with my brother's family for a summer.

After I painted my brother's house, I ended up going back to live in CT with my family. Slowly, I began watching TV to pass the time, and I began to eat more and put on weight. One fact that I should reiterate is that when I was traveling across the country, I was barely eating and I ended up losing a lot of weight. When I initially moved back in with my parents, I really had no appetite and was underweight. At times, I was even disgusted by chewing and swallowing.

Even as I began to lose myself in television, I still was experiencing Ella talking to me. Every night, I would go to bed and try and just stop thinking and just hear a constant stream of consciousness from Ella. Sometimes, I tried just to listen; sometimes, I couldn't resist chiming in, and other times, I continued to try and improve Ella's vocabulary and grammar.

This led to a roller-coaster ride of stories and closeted "delusional" thinking, which culminated in me eventually being overwhelmed and just surrendering to Ella and trying to just do what she said. It was winter in the early morning when I finally gave in, and she told me to get naked and go outside. I took off my clothes and started walking down the street naked.

I didn't get far before somebody saw me and called the police. The police took me to an ambulance, and I ended up being admitted to a psych ward for the second time. Apparently, my parents didn't know where I went at first and were completely taken by surprise that I had been found walking naked down the road. All I remember from being in the hospital was that I was incredibly scared of dealing with the nurses. I don't recall if I admitted to hearing Ella at that time, but I know I was put on some antipsychotics, and they seemed to help.

The progress at which this insidious process of being lured into following commands took a long time. I was constantly interacting with voices in between daily activities. I was not really doing anything other than the occasional chore and watching television. This behavior went on for months and slowly wore away my ability to resist the voices. I imagine this is what others go through a slow wearing away of resistance to voices. Resisting the lure of voices takes, energy, maintenance, and is helped by support. I was not doing anything to maintain my sanity, instead my agency was being eroded by the lack of support, the isolation, and the fact that my emotional needs were not being met.

30 RETELLING AS "WE"

In January or February of 2011, we found ourselves back in our childhood home. We had exhausted most of our cash reserves. We had stopped paying bills despite having multiple credit cards and a leased truck. We stopped paying for our cell phone and so we cut ourselves off from all our friends, and we stopped communicating via e-mail. There were traces of us and ways to get in contact with us like Facebook and LinkedIn accounts, but only two people from our time in Rhode Island would actually make an effort to contact us.

In our parents' home, we found ourselves pretty shell-shocked from our journey across the country and the bombardment of voices. As we were trying to sort through the debris left over from our mental escapades, our daily activities became rather mundane. Our parents were retired and worked sporadically, so most of our time was spent on the couch in front of the TV. We spent many desperate weeks with nothing to do, and we tended to just sit and observe all types of delusional thoughts and imagery travel through our mind's eye as we sat pretending to watch TV. We recall just sitting in front of the TV and having no interest in what was on. We just sat and observed the madness that had crept into our lives.

There were signs of Chance in there, trying to come to terms with what happened and trying to figure out what steps to take in order to move on. We would end up looking at job postings and even brainstormed about starting another painting company, but in reality, we were mentally overwhelmed and tenuously holding on to sanity. We are amazed and yet not surprised that our parents just let us stay in this state with little interference or advice. We do not blame them for the role they played because they really had no idea what was going on in our head and the mental escapades that played out. However, we do admit that it was obvious that something was severely wrong, and our family way of dealing with it was not to confront the blaring possibility that Chance was teetering on the edge.

Our personal way of dealing with the confusion was to shut down for the most part. As we spent our days hibernating inside our minds, we slowly did start to figure that we had to do something. So when spring started to come along, we ended up pursuing the opportunity to painting the interior of our brother's new house. We stayed up in New Hampshire for days. Our brother had a girlfriend and a baby girl named Alice, and we spent time with them.

We would go alone and work on the new house. We found that work was a good distraction, but our mind was still a circus and we were starting to have conversations with voices that were really causing us frustration. For one thing, since everybody treated us like nothing was wrong, we figured that there must not be something wrong with what we were going through. The madness that was inherent in our heads was not making waves, so it seemed totally normal to us. So, we just kept it in for the most part until one night at my brother's new house.

We don't recall why, but one night at our brother's new house during work we found ourselves screaming in the bathroom. We were all alone in the house, and we were pissed about what was happening to us. If anybody had come to the house that night, they would have found me screaming obscenities at the mirror and frantically ranting and raving up and down the hallways of the house for over an hour. But alas, when I finally had blown up, I was still alone. Eventually we tired ourselves out, but we remember seeing small pixel-like faces in the windows, watching us, and felt like we were a spectacle to behold.

All through the night and into the next morning, we recall lying in bed and hearing the furnace come on and strange bells ringing in the house. They could have been hallucinations because at the time, the voices were trying to convince us to just leave everything behind and just walk away from our life. We really were fighting to hold on to our identity as Chance and had it in our mind that if we did leave, we would be lost forever. We thought that if we did leave, we would literally transform into another being and we would be swallowed by the voices and the world.

There was an inherent fear of the unknown and the ultimate goals of the voices. It did seem like we were a very lucky person, and despite our many transgressions in the physical and spiritual, we were being somehow protected from danger. We were torn as to whether to leave our family or not. We don't know if this was an issue with just going out into the world and making our own way, or if there was something else at hand. Either way, our choice was to go back toward safety. This especially was due to our fundamental understanding that hearing the voices and having all of these sensory experiences made us believe that if we were to leave everything and not look back, we would end up in a psych ward again. That feeling was coming from the logical perspective of what we knew was going on in our mind and how we thought others would see us as a crazy person.

This logical perception kept us from doing violent or dangerous things, but it would be tested time and time again as events rolled on. And time rolled on slowly. After we worked on our brother's house, we ended up back at home again, and our parents did something very reasonable: they asked for rent money. At the time, we were in financial ruin and didn't really even have access to a bank account, and so we talked to our brother and he invited us to go live in New Hampshire in the new house.

We ended up going to live in New Hampshire because we didn't have to pay rent there. Our brother spoke to his friends at work and asked around if anybody needed painting done. We spent weeks helping around the house and playing with our niece on a daily basis. We watched TV and spoke to our voices and kept very tight-lipped about what was going on in our inner world. We were constantly thinking back to the more vivid details of our psychedelic and hallucinogenic visions and trying to make meaning of them in an obsessive manner. We overturned the details of our narrative ruthlessly and came up with all types of delusional explanations with the voices about how we were changing the world and how we could all do miraculous things and how powerful and wonderful we were. How the visions and what we saw in our dreams were laying a path for the future.

Of course, we kept all the grandiosity to ourselves and played the part of the humble poor loser that could not get out of his own way. We kept it all in, and despite the universe finding ways to give us a support net of sorts, it didn't seem to fully support the narrative that was constantly playing out in our mind and connecting events, people, and visions to give us a semblance of a logical story that made sense as to what our circumstances had become and how far we felt we had fallen.

31 NEW HAMPSHIRE

When we moved to New Hampshire, it was summer, and we were waiting around to do house-painting projects. We worked on and off into the fall. We spent our time talking about very superficial things with our brother and his girlfriend, and we spent a lot of time playing with our niece and making a lot of pillow forts. Despite being welcomed into our brother's house, we still kept the alternative realities, voices, and madness to ourselves. If we were not working or watching TV, we were most likely rehashing and reworking all of the visions and psychedelic experiences that we had and trying to integrate new dreams into a narrative that made life make sense.

The setting of a suburban home where the focus of the day was just mundane living was not the best place for us to really make any progress on our narrative. In fact, it exacerbated it because the everyday life that our brother, niece, and his girlfriend were living was utterly at odds with the wild and imaginative inner life we were living. Our inner and outer lives were not harmonious at all.

When we were painting houses, we were alone for the most part, and we had convinced ourselves that we didn't have to breathe in order to live. So, we held our breath for long periods of time and took very shallow breaths. We breathed as little as possible, regardless of whether we were working or just relaxing, watching television. This was just another artifact that was suggested to us through visions and voices, but it stuck with us and still has meaning today.

After a few months living at our brother's house, we had made about three thousand dollars painting other people's houses, and we were considering what else we could do to make money because we figured it was vital to make money in order to live. But after painting the houses, we found ourselves with a lot of time, to rehash our journey in isolation. Every day the fact that we were talking to voices when nobody was paying attention started to catch up with us.

One afternoon in the fall time, we decided to take a walk and leave everything behind. As we left, the voices told us not to take anything, but we had the cash from painting the houses, so we pocketed it, figuring that we would be able to start a new life in a different state with this money. It would pay for an apartment or some other shelter while we got situated in our new life. We left our brother's house with a T-shirt and a flannel shirt and some long pants and just started to walk north. The voices had been telling us that we needed to be cold for months and so we figured we would just keep walking north.

After about thirty minutes of walking, we decided that we wanted a new identity, so we took the money out of our wallet and threw our ID and wallet away. Then we threw our keys away and just walked away. We don't recall exactly what we thought about as we walked north, but at that point, we were hearing voices in the sounds of cars driving by, and it seemed like the volume of the cars going by depended on what we were thinking about. What we mean to say is that sometimes the sounds of the traffic whizzing by would get incredibly intense and seem angry, and other times, it would quiet down, depending on our train of thought. We left midmorning and just kept walking on roads we weren't familiar with all afternoon without any food or water.

As evening closed in and things started to get dark, it also got colder. We were freezing but just kept going, and we started to see things in the world around us. At one point in the darkness when we looked at the trees, we could see giant ants frozen in place in the canopies in the trees. They were not moving; it was like walking through a world of frozen giants in the treetops. At the same time when we looked at the side of the road, we saw grass like plants that would move when we looked at them. If we stared too long, they would begin to move and grow to reach out toward us.

At the point where we started to notice these visual anomalies, we also started to perceive the dark around us as a living thing. And that's when we started to see the darkness around us actually manifesting itself into a holographic cloud made up of tiny abstract shapes and objects. When we stopped walking, we could actually see the darkness come alive all around us, and it seemed that we were walking through a tunnel of darkness and it would close in around us when we stopped walking. At one point, we even saw it reaching out intelligently to touch us as if in a caress. This manifestation occurred all night long as we walked and was consistently haunting.

At the time, we were amazed and bewildered by what we were seeing, but we just kept walking through the tunnel of darkness through the unknown countryside of New Hampshire. We were cold and hungry, and at some point in the night, a police officer pulled over next to us and invited us to the police station. We went with him and sat indoors, warming up and trying to doze for about an hour, before we drank some water and headed back out.

At that point after seeing all the visions and having some weird perceptual issues about seeing street signs in the dark, we decided that we should turn around and go home. The only catch was that during the day we had decided at some point that the voices were right and we didn't need any money. We dropped over three thousand dollars in hundred-dollar bills on the side of the road. Hopefully, some soul in need found that money, and it enriched their lives.

We spent the rest of the night walking south, trying to retrace our steps with voices that were not happy that we had abandoned our plan. We managed to navigate south by a different route and ended up near where we had thrown our keys and wallet by early the next morning. We retrieved our personal belongings and continued our inward and outward journey back to our brother's house and were eventually flagged down by another police officer. This time, the officer saw us and put us in his car and drove us to meet up with our brother. We got in the car with our brother and went home without many questions asked. We just said we decided to go for a walk, and that was that.

At this point, we don't know what our family was thinking. If they worried, they didn't outwardly show much concern to us, so we just went on as we had been, talking to voices, imagining what our narrative meant, and trying to integrate what happened and what was happening into a perceptive framework we could wrap our head around. As the days grew short and winter approached, the voices got worse and worse. After we failed to walk away from life again, we were in a constant fight with the voices to convince them that everything was OK and that we were going to eventually have a wondrous life even though in the short run the opposite looked to be true.

We would have long conversations where we would talk for hours about all the positive things we could do and draw from inspirational people in our lives and try to convince the voices that everything would be great. The voices would go along for a while and then become increasingly negative and loud and commanding. The more we talked to voices, the more they dominated our attention, and the harder it was to live the mundane family life that the people around us were living.

Finally, one night we were unable to fall asleep; we spent all night arguing with voices, going back and forth about how wonderful and horrible life was. By the early morning, we were getting really worn down and desperate. It seemed that no matter what we said and how convincing our arguments were, the voices would agree for a while and then turn on us. Eventually we gave up on trying to convince the voices that everything was going to be all right and that we could control ourselves. Once again, the voices told us to get naked and go outside and just leave. We gave up and did just that.

We got naked and went downstairs and walked right past my brother's girlfriend on the couch. We went outside and walked down the street naked and headed for the main road. My brother's girlfriend got my brother up, and they drove over to us and got a blanket around us and brought us to be checked out.

We ended up in some type of doctor's office that had a waiting room next to a large office area. we recall seeing the doctor and having my attention split. We were trying to pay attention to the doctor, but every time we had any thoughts to our self we were seeing something that was very distressing. We could see streams of information coming down from above us and affecting all of the workers in the office. Every time we thought we observed the activity in the office pausing as if to listen. Then when we went blank and stopped thinking there would be a flurry of information coming in from above and we would perceive that we were somehow influencing reality with my thoughts.

We talked to a doctor and they asked us if we wanted to go to the hospital. We were freaked out and just decided to go with the flow. We ended up going for a stay in another mental hospital.

In the hospital in New Hampshire, we ended up staying for about a week. We don't remember a lot of what went on there, but we did end up taking medication, which quelled the voices pretty quickly. We vividly remember talking to another woman patient who was surprisingly positive and happy and seemed to be convinced that she was a doctor. This woman knew she was in treatment but seemed to behave as though she was a doctor herself. We found this odd, but she was pleasant so we talked to her and the other patients. The other thing we remember about that facility was the outdoor space that we were allowed to spend time in maybe once in our entire stay. We were encouraged to play games and have fun, but only for like thirty minutes for one day during the entire stay.

Staying at the facility in New Hampshire was not very eventful, but it did get us on medication, and when we were finally discharged, there were follow-up appointments made with a psychiatrist in NH. The most important event that happened is that a social worker got us to apply for Medicaid so that our hospital bill would be covered and we would get some type of health care.

We left the hospital with a prescription and started taking medication every day, and the voices seemed to calm down. We don't remember much happening after the stay in the hospital, and we hung around in NH for a few more months. Eventually, we started to go to the psychiatrist, and we were given medication and more appointments. Our Medicaid didn't cover every expense incurred by the psychiatrist, so they told us to apply for disability.

Around that time, our brother started to try and talk to us about what we were going to be doing with our lives. He told us that if we were going to stay at his house, we would have to pay rent. Then our parents came up to visit, and we took the opportunity to move back in with them. This complicated things because our doctor was in New Hampshire. But we didn't have any money and any job prospects, so we moved back to Connecticut.

32 LIVING WITH THE BOILING UNDERCURRENT

After we moved back to Monroe, we found ourselves medicated on an antipsychotic called Risperdal. This drug was effective at keeping our voices at bay, but it had a side effect that made life very frustrating. We only could concentrate on any one subject for ten minutes before feeling an overwhelming feeling of restlessness and the need to change activities. This meant that we could no longer really read or watch television to pass the time. Seeing as reading and television were the foundation of our daily activity, we soon found the excuse to go off medication. It did take almost a year, but we eventually stopped taking medication and resumed speaking with voices.

Our doctor was in New Hampshire, and we were visiting them when we had appointments. But by early spring the following year, we stopped going to the appointments. On some level, we thought the medication had done its job and we were functioning fairly normally. We stopped medication but really had no follow-up on how we were behaving, and we kept our experiences from our parents as we lived at home.

Eventually the voices started creeping back in slowly. Again, we found ourselves trying to rally the voices to our side to help us and be congruent with a vision for a positive future. The voices seemed swayed by our arguments at first, but if we relented even the tiniest bit moving in a positive direction or had any setback that changed our positive outlook, we were immediately plunged into conflicting dialogue with the voices.

We kept just wearing ourselves out convincing the voices that things would be OK, and when we grew tired of the effort to keep the voices in check, they took advantage and started trying to convince us to do irrational things. They would not divulge why they wanted to do these things or what their overall purpose was, which only persuaded us to doggedly try to get the voices' confidence so that we could better understand what they were and what they were trying to accomplish.

By this point, we remember waking up from dreams and hearing wild and fantastic stories about what was happening in our life that involved everything from aliens, to godly beings, and all types of connections that the voices would start to elucidate about. When the voices started to go off on a wild fantastical explanation, we would cut them off before the narrative grew too wild and rein them in. We constantly tried to bring the focus back to the fact that the voices could support us in our efforts to heal by just being loving and congruent, but they were wildly imaginative beings that had personality of their own and did not want to be boxed. So our dance continued.

One morning, we were sitting outside on the deck in the warm sun and fighting our inner battle against the voices. For some reason, our frustration boiled over and we began yelling. When we yelled, we were so loud that we heard the echo of our voice bouncing off the surroundings. We took this to support the belief that we could be heard by the surrounding neighbors every time we thought and at every utterance. We thought that the echo was proof of our voices being projected around the country and maybe even the world.

We had harbored the suspicion that we were being monitored by observers, which had caused us great confusion and self-scrutiny at times. The feeling that our thoughts could be heard had crushed our feeling of privacy and left us feeling vulnerable and ashamed of all of the alternative thoughts that we had. On one hand, we thought that since our minds were not private, we should be ashamed of lewd or crude thoughts; but on the other hand, we felt provoked to act out so that if we were being observed, those who observed us would see our defiance against the lack of privacy. The conflict between the shame of having lurid thoughts and feeling as though we should actively police our own thoughts had existed for some time but came to a head that day when we heard our voice echo in the backyard.

At the moment we perceived personal proof we could project our voice so loudly that we could be heard, we really lost it. The irony is that we had to yell to be heard and that we were keeping all our thoughts that we wanted to be heard to ourselves. We ultimately snapped and came into the house, ranting and raving. Our mother seemed alarmed, and we vented our frustration at her; when she didn't have any words of consolation for us, we walked over to her and grabbed her by the shoulders and moved her around the room forcibly with no intent to harm her. We were trying to show her that she could control herself and move about freely by manipulating her to move herself. It was most likely one of our first attempts to show our mother that she was able to exert more control on the world and possibly even give us attention that we desperately needed.

Then we walked out to the garage and took a sledgehammer and just wanted to destroy something, so we started to hit our newly bought snow blower. It was a used snow blower, and we dented the hood and far from destroyed the machine. After we had exerted a bit of control on our life, we walked down to a rock in the front yard and just sat waiting for the ambulance to come. We had overheard our mother calling the police, and we did not want to actually harm another being; we just wanted to destroy the situation we were witnessing and fused to.

The ambulance came, and a number of paramedics came up to us and started to talk to us. We recall vividly that our emotions were cycling from desire to fear to happiness, and we felt like we couldn't control or regulate how we felt toward the paramedics. They were kind, and we did end up voluntarily getting in the ambulance. It struck us that some part of our psyche was in turmoil because it was like the unconscious processes of our mind were malfunctioning while we keenly observed the effects. For the most part, we just felt dumbfounded.

On the ambulance ride to the hospital, we calmed down and felt calmer and calmer. By the time we got to the hospital, our crisis had passed, and our need for control had subsided. The voices had also calmed down. We were brought into an examining room after a while, and the nurse told us to take off our clothes and put on a gown. At this point, we felt pretty good and decided that we just wanted to go home. We refused to change, and we requested that we be allowed to leave. The nurse responded by getting male attendants and holding the door shut so that we could not leave. There was no lock on the door, and for about thirty seconds, we felt caged and tried to push the door open.

The attendants eventually forced their way into the room and forcibly put me onto a gurney. A very nice nurse came into the room, and I told her that I did not consent to being admitted and that I just wanted to go home. She told me that there was an alternative: I could sign a piece of paper, and everything would be taken care of. I trusted her kindness, but in reality, she had just gotten me to sign over my rights to be admitted to another psychiatric facility that was associated with the hospital that was twice as expensive.

We were transported to the new facility in Westport, where we were given a private room and told that we had to stay in our room while our stay was processed. We waited in that room and eventually went to bed. Late that night, a strange event happened. Apparently, another patient had been admitted, and he ran down the hall and opened the door to our room and yelled, "Chance! I have been looking for you!" We had been lying sleeplessly in bed and this patient came into the room and clasped hands with us like he knew who we were. Immediately, orderlies came into the room and pulled us apart. We both wrestled to stay together, and we instantly felt a connection to this patient who somehow knew our name. The orderlies forcibly wrapped us back in our bed and gave us a sedative, and we relaxed into a daze, trying to figure out what it meant that this naked stranger knew our name.

The next day, we immediately found this patient. We don't recall his name at this point, but it seemed like he came from a wealthy family and he was accustomed to acting out, to the dislike of his conservative family. We immediately started playing chess and reading poetry together when we got the chance, in order to pass the time. When we were not with him, we recall speaking to voices and having thoughts that our body was covered in tiny wormholes that were microscopic and connected to different parts of the universe. We had some bizarre thoughts, and we did a lot of yoga and stretching in addition to just staring into space for long periods of time.

We didn't like the common room because whenever we were around groups of people, we felt uncomfortable and ended up just sitting and staring silently at the ground while we sensed energy and activity surging all around us. We easily could comprehend how some people diagnosed with schizophrenia seem to just go into a trance and become unresponsive. In our own experience, being completely still would allow us to observe an invisible world that we perceived all around us, where we could sense activities beyond sight and sound.

After the first few days, we started to take medication regularly and got settled in as our voices dissipated and our thoughts returned to normal. At first, taking the medication caused us to feel like a demon had taken control of our body and was inflicting symptoms that we couldn't control on our neck and back, but soon we began to accept the side effects of the antipsychotics.

We have some bizarre recollections of other mental patients doing some miraculous things, like an old man that was in his room having orderlies and nurses swarm him because he was being difficult, and then seeing him a moment later on the other side of the facility, walking as if nothing had happened. And one day as we played cards with that man, we felt a haze of disorderly thinking and confusion descend upon us, and we don't know if it was our confusion or if we were sensing the disorderly nature of his mind.

We ended up making friends, talking to strangers, and participating in group activities, which helped pass the time, but nobody seemed to show any sign that they knew what we were going through mentally. The first time we saw our psychiatrist, he started asking us questions. While we were paying attention, he started to speak gibberish, and we felt a presence descended on the room. We followed the strange gibberish he used and then we remember him saying, "He doesn't get it" afterward. This just made us more paranoid that some veiled secret was being kept from us.

Eventually we were released from the facility, and we had a few phone numbers of patients that we met, but we didn't hear from them and we still were afraid to share anything deep about what was happening in our minds. The naked guy from the first night we had befriended even remarked to us before we left, "How do you do it?" We don't know if he was talking about just coping with reality or putting up the front that we were OK despite the very real feeling that there was something seriously wrong with our world.

We ended up going home with a prescription for about thirty days, but no real follow-up. We had had one breakthrough, or so we thought, with our parents during our stay. When they came to visit for the first time, we had gotten really emotional and so had they and we felt as though they understood us in the moment, but they only really showed empathy and the way they felt upset because of the situation we were in that one time. Every other time they would show their emotions about the situation our lives had become, they seemed to be indifferent or just plain frustrated.

33 TO THE HOSPITAL!

Time moved on, the medication mediated the voices, and then without any follow up our medication ran out. We experienced a period of stability for a few months where we vegetated and then the same cycle played over again. The voices started to creep in and take over our attention. We really had nothing to distract from hearing voices because they could manifest themselves in music, in television, and in sound itself. So, the voices came back once again and dominated life and took over reality.

Eventually one morning after going back and forth with the voices for over a month, we found ourselves once again sleepless and arguing with the voices all night. By the early morning, we once again gave in to the voices' commands to get naked and go outside and just leave. At the time, we were so fused and consumed by the process of arguing with voices that we didn't even realize what was happening. In the moment, we just gave in and took a walk completely naked in the early winter morning.

Our parents were not awake yet, so this time, we walked a couple hundred yards toward the main road before we were reported to the police. The police just drove us to the police station and transferred us to an ambulance, which then brought us to a local hospital where we were admitted to the mental ward for observation. During our stay at the ward, we kept to our self and didn't really participate with other patients. We took medication and slowly recovered from hearing voices, but we recall vividly that whenever our blood pressure and heart rate were taken, our pulse was always racing and our senses were all heightened. We awoke at every little noise and were startled by the constant opening and closing of doors.

Eventually, we were once again discharged, and now we were referred to a local community agency that would give us a transitional psychiatrist and attempt to keep us medicated. At that time, we were told that we most likely suffered from bipolar-I disorder, and despite the fact that we had admitted to doctors that we heard voices, the doctors did not admit to us that we had symptoms associated with schizophrenia.

Even after we started seeing a psychiatrist at the GBMHC, he did not disclose what particular condition we were suffering from. He did admit to us that we should just be happy that we had a class of drugs to treat what was happening to us. We went many months symptom-free for the most part, but daily living was not tolerable or sustainable in the long run on Risperdal because we couldn't really focus on any given activity for more than ten to fifteen minutes. We think that it was about this time that we told our psychiatrist that we would like to try a different medication. He suggested haloperidol with the addition of Cogentin in order to treat the Parkinson's-like symptoms that using haloperidol caused.

The transformation from hearing voices to not was immediate. However, our psychiatrist told us that we were very sick and that we should apply for disability. The GBMHC arranged for us to meet with a specialist that helped patients sign up for disability. We applied and our application was successful. We were legally disabled and started to receive disability benefits monthly starting in early 2012.

Why did we need to be on disability? Well, the haloperidol and Cogentin had an interesting set of side effects. We no longer heard voices, and we could read and watch television better than when we were on Risperdal, but we also stayed in bed between twelve and sixteen hours a day. When we took the Cogentin, it made us need to lie down; we didn't always sleep but instead lay around with the feeling of being comfortable and feeling a strange sensation not to do anything. We still thought, and at night sometimes, we heard voices. We dreamt wild imaginative and provocative dreams that we could barely remember after waking. The new medication was nearly completely masking all of the symptoms we had before, but it also left us disabled and confused about what future we had.

34 ALONE

Isolation was a huge part of our life. We are at the point in our personal story where we experienced the kind of social isolation that many people with disturbances experience. Being cut off from friends that one can share with and not experiencing support on an emotional level was once our norm. We were technically disabled for three years. During the time from 2012 to 2015, we hung out with friends from high school and college twice. Our family did not push us to get a job once we had been placed on disability, nor did they in any way encourage us to fight for our life. We were enabled to just exist and deal with the circumstances that said we were just disordered and, on some level, life just stopped developing.

Our medication was keeping us from hearing voices for the majority of the day, but it was also crippling us by keeping us in bed. We became clinically depressed and really had no hobbies or daily activities other than television, reading nonfiction, the occasional chore, and living fantasies in our head to cope with the crushing isolation and boredom. It may sound great to have three years off, but let me tell you, it was tortuous when our only getaway was to see family that had no words of encouragement or validation for us. We can only imagine what other people go through to cope with a place of helplessness like we were in.

We stopped showering regularly and didn't really brush our teeth. We started to wake up after noon and stay up past 2 in the morning if we were able to stay awake. Some days when we were feeling especially comfortable in bed, we would just stay in bed past 3 p.m. or 4 p.m. During the summer our father would occasionally have projects planned for us and we would get up at 9 a.m., but even then, some days it would take us an hour or more to get out of bed.

For those years of life, we don't have many specific memories. We recall thinking about death and how just ending everything would be a godsend.

Sitting in bed and loathing our circumstances happened now and again, but for the most part the medication just made us feel dumbed down, fuzzy, and numb. We did not have motivation to do anything for the most part. Every chore made us feel like procrastinating, and over time we started to really question if this was going to be the way the rest of our life was lived.

There was another reason why we were so unhappy; after we got out of the last hospital stay, we were treated at the GBCMH center, but they were a transitional community center. After a few months with them, we had to find a psychiatrist that we could see regularly. The doctors were concerned because we had been in and out of mental institutions four times now in Kentucky, New Hampshire, and Connecticut. We found an outpatient program called REACH that had a psychiatrist that we could see, and we started to make appointments regularly.

Now we have gotten the notes from our psychiatry appointments, and the doctors described us as hostile and incapable of being evaluated for the most part. We still do not know why the doctors perceived us as being "incapable" of being evaluated. But we will say this, we spent fifteen minutes with these professionals about once every ninety days. Every time we visited them, they went through a list of questions that they had to ask, which took up most of the visit. These were the stock questions like "Have you had thoughts of harming yourself?" or "Have you heard voices?" or "Have you had any homicidal thoughts?"

Never once did they ask us if we felt supported or if we felt loved or if we felt isolated or if we were scared about life. Doctors never asked us if we had fantasies or delusions. Doctors never treated us like we were capable of standing on our own two feet, or even validated our experience as being human. We wouldn't even find out that we were diagnosed as schizophrenic for years; when we asked what our symptoms were, we were told we were being treated for bipolar I. Years later a psychiatrist would comment to us, "The meds you are on aren't even for bipolar . . . They are antipsychotics."

We realize now that the responsibility to get better mostly lay in our own hands. The current system does have a safety net in place to keep people manageable and even dormant, in some regards. If a person with symptoms does not want to get better or know how to get better, unless somebody puts their neck out and supports them, then that person will have to pull themselves up. The system is a safety net. If you fall, there is somebody there to catch you, but currently you can sit in the net and stay in limbo, or if you want something better, you'll have to climb out yourself.

We would have loved to find some reason to find motivation earlier in the past eight years, but unfortunately, we did not find serious motivation until 2016. Some of it had to do with parts of our safety net being removed, and other parts had to do with just feeling sick and tired and afraid of being nothing. We did not want to live on the edges of society and continue being isolated from others. Strangely enough, medication and voices became the combined ingredients to finding our motivation, but that process started around 2014.

35 AWARENESS

While we languished, we were still completely aware of what we were losing day in and day out as we just sat around watching television in an attempt to distance ourselves from our trauma. We had known hundreds of people as friends, and we knew they were all moving on with their lives as we sat paralyzed by our inability to communicate. We constantly thought about our friends from Rhode Island and UCONN and high school, what they were doing, who they were marrying, if they were having kids. We hibernated through birthdays, anniversaries, holidays, and countless reminders that we were going nowhere.

We can count the number of times we saw friends from 2011 to the end of 2016. Twice. We hung out with a group of friends twice, and we initiated the hangout both times. We celebrated one birthday with friends in five years. After we actively reaching out to people, they didn't even bother to contact us back after hanging out. We felt as if our old world had moved on from us. It seemed as if we were being rejected by the world because two people we met out of dozens reached out to us over the course of five years.

We had been making our "friends" thousands and thousands of dollars in Rhode Island. We had put ourselves through so much stress and paranoia and danger because the bigger we had gotten in Rhode Island, the more we felt like people were depending on us. The truth is that a lot of the people we met in Rhode Island, college, and high school were not actually interested in who we had been, but more in what we offered them. There was a give-and-take in relationships and in our past relationships, we had set a precedent that we just gave our all for others. Even now we feel like in a lot of relationships, we find that we give more than others.

We feel as though we have a lot to give, and we tend to give ourselves away freely because that is how we would like to see other people in the world act. To give their vulnerabilities away, to share their experiences and thoughts that they never have discussed. We want people to be able to share their traumas and their joys equally and be free in the ways that we have felt free in the last months since November. We see how other people bottle themselves up and disconnect from their potential because they never were taught properly how to connect to the world. Our vast connection to reality did cripple us for years, but what we went through was a lesson that had been etched in stone for us.

We believe talking about the simple preventative teaching and screening measures we have been thinking about seem trivial when stated but are deeply powerful tools that could be harnessed to the benefit of others that are struggling. The only measure we don't think we have talked about is the need to screen children, adolescents, and adults for isolation and loneliness. This is one of the common factors we have encountered whenever reading about people with a schizophrenic condition, and we would not be surprised if isolation and loneliness were prevalent in many other cases of mental disorder.

We believe the profound knowledge of connection in this world could help prevent the scourge of mental illness. The large body of current work and historical events that supports the concepts of the interwoven fabric of the collective narrative of reality should sound a call to arms. We should be arming every student, patient, and person in the world with academic research, spiritual practice, education, or historical records that point to the importance of the intertwining connections of this world. More importantly we should be teaching youth and those afflicted how to interpret their lives and access information about what reality really consists of in order to improve our human existence.

36 MEDICATION MANAGEMENT

In the years that we were disabled and even following, we really thought about other people a lot, but were so distracted by our circumstances, symptoms, and side effects of medicine that we mostly focused on ourselves. We had many thoughts of going back to dealing because the money was so good. We were tempted badly to reconnect with our old acquaintances, but in the end, we decided to remain isolated from the catalysts that felt like enablers for bad decision making.

Instead we stopped taking care of ourselves and became depressed and resigned for some time. We spent the majority of our time watching television and reading fiction. We took every opportunity to escape from the reality that we had come to find unbearable without the understanding of what role the voices and miraculous events meant about our identity and reality's purpose. We stopped bathing and brushing our teeth, and our family would complain now and again and try to shame us into taking care of ourselves.

We did not really experience any compassion or sense of understanding from anybody, so we just stayed isolated. With the urging of our psychiatrist, we fluctuated our medication in order to see if it would be possible to come off medication. We experimented over and over, coming off medication, and every time voices would gradually grow stronger and stronger as we reduced the medication.

We started getting used to a pattern of hearing voices for about a month then going back on medication for a few months, then tapering the medication and trying to reduce our intake. After three years we felt like we were learning from the voices, but they were not changing from their pattern of teetering back and forth from support to prosecution and command. After years of trying, we still attempted to educate the voices and correct and play devil's advocate with them as we replayed the events of our dreams and journey in our head. We were constantly reframing our understanding of reality in bizarre and obscure ways that could sound delusional because they were based on connections we were making between literature, movies, television, and our lives.

Fantasy and entertainment was our only real outlets at the time, so we started defining reality by the positive messages and stories that our daily life was drenched in. Our tenuous grasp on the world was nurtured by the connections we formed in fantasy and by our young niece whom we visited often. She was the only person in our family that did not know or was capable of not completely understanding our circumstances. She was innocent and allowed us to interact with another human being without judgment.

She was a light in dark times, and despite the feeling like spending time with her could be work or frustrating at times, we were able to let down our guard and play and act genuinely with her. We began to feel love for another being and cherished the only relationship that we really had, which was completely devoid of any fear of judgment. This relationship was the outlet which would help us poke our head out of our shell and feel like we were a human being. Otherwise we really just felt like a burden and a problem.

After three long years on disability, we had to reapply, so we filled out the forms and sent in our application, but we were denied. We were paying rent to our parents, and we were trying to figure out a method to make money because we had savings, but they would not last forever. After a few months on medication and feeling like we needed to do something to get back into society, we decided to look into getting a job. We looked around and went on one interview, but we really could not find any position that would pay a decent living salary. So, we decided we would just go for whatever we could.

We ended up interviewing for a sales associate position at a large warehouse building supply company in the winter of 2015. We went to the interview and easily got a job. We were hired as a part-time employee starting in early 2016. Surprisingly this was a great idea. Because of this decision, we would end up meeting friends and be reintroduced to the social niceties of life.

37 BACK TO WORK

In our first week on the job, we ended up meeting Antoni, who is one of our best friends now. He walked up to me at work one of the first days and said, "Have you ever done PCP?" To this day it is still the oddest introduction we have ever had in life, and it still brings a smile to our face. We were not completely sure about befriending this strange man, but we made plans to hang out and we ended up spending a lot of time together.

He is the first person that we decided we would tell our story to. We would tell him story after story of drugs, money, sex, adventures, and everything bizarre. We opened up the spigot, and it just all flowed out. The more we shared, the better we felt. At that time, we had been growing a beard for two years, so our face was scruffy and people compared us to Vikings and commented on our facial hair a lot. Secretly we were really hiding behind the facial hair, but something about sharing started some kind of momentum that was unstoppable.

We met Antoni's friends and got to know them little by little over time. They did not get the whole story behind us, but we would drop a lot of hints about what happened to us and we were not shy about discussing voices, drugs, hallucinations, or funny fantastic stories. We were odd but had a lot of material. We really did not have anything else to talk about because all we had done for the last four or five years was watch television and spend time with our boring family.

As we worked at the building warehouse, we found ourselves bored by the work but enriched because we had the opportunity to talk to people and actually help do something for a change. After we worked for a few months, a contractor named Ivan came into the department we worked in and asked us if we knew anybody that was looking for a part-time job. He said he could use help a few days a week. We said we would ask around and took his card. After another month of working part-time and trying to figure out what we could do, we decided to call Ivan and see if he still needed help.

Ivan asked us to go to his house and do some very easy work to try us out. We were pretty capable at that point and breezed through the work. So now we worked at the building warehouse a few days a week and for Ivan on our days off. Working full time allowed us to start saving, and around the same time we started to more and more seriously consider what our future held. We knew we could start a company and make decent money, but our confidence in making a living devoted to monetary profits was really injured. We wanted to do something worthwhile that would actually seem worthwhile and fulfilling, unlike our job as a sales associate and as an assistant to a contractor.

Now as we got to know Ivan, we actually found him to be a brilliantly wise man under his gruff exterior. Despite the fact that he tended to isolate himself to the company of family and clients, he had an amazingly huge heart and esoteric knowledge of an alternative viewpoint that was both wise and exotic. When we began to explain our history to Ivan, we were surprised that he totally was interested in our visions and alternative experiences and he even had theories about what and who we were. He totally accepted us for our experience, and he began to share about himself.

Ivan believed in spirituality, astral projection, mediation, healing, Jesus, angels, aliens, and he found his knowledge through alternative means than big media. Ivan studied teachings of many wise men and gurus that had explanations of creation, reality, and how it was constructed. Ivan took different aspects of teaching and applied what resonated with him to his beliefs. Before he explained anything about different dimensions or higher beings or meditation, he always said it was OK if we did not believe what he said because we each had our own ideas of reality or matrixes that we created, which defined our own realities.

As we shared more and more with Ivan and Antoni, we found outlets to start processing what happened to us out loud. We found compassion, understanding, and the validation that it was OK to talk about the voices. As the year grew to a close, we had decided that we were going to try and go to school to get our physical therapy degree. We knew that physical therapists made great money and helped people heal. We were thirty-four at the time and knew that we could still join the army and get the GI bill to pay for school. So, we decided that on the first day of 2017, we decided to go off medication. We figured we had been medicated for almost a year with very few symptoms. We felt like we were moving forward toward something positive. We had friends and felt like we were growing again.

38 PROCESSING LIFE BY SHARING

The change in perspective toward growth did not happen overnight. We had suffered disability and were coming out of the fog of sleep and inactivity when we began working at the builder's warehouse in 2016. It had been a long hard road to that point, but things were looking up. After we met Antoni, we began to hang out with him and go out to get a drink now and again and we began to talk about ourselves with Antoni. Talking about what we had gone through and what was on our mind with complete transparency did not come right away.

At first, we began telling wild stories of daring and defiance of the laws. We told about funny stories of altered states of mind and the calamity that followed them around. We talked about women and friends and employees and all the characters that we had met. We were quite lucid and medicated at that time, and so we really began reflecting on our behaviors and touched on the mysterious experiences. In turn Antoni told us about his life and family, and we learned what he had been through.

There was no judgment about our experiences being crazy, delusional, or a symptom of mental health. There was just a bond of sharing our experiences, and this was a learning experience that we will never forget after years of isolation and festering thoughts and suspicions.

Working at the builder's warehouse with Antoni was not all fun. We were working a job as a rental sales associate, and we were responsible for taking care of customers and taking payments while processing rentals. The job was not challenging really; it was busy work to start earning a paycheck. The managers seemed eager to hire us because we were intelligent and had a degree and even tried to rope us into working on becoming more involved in the store.

What we came to realize is that we could perform any menial job and much more complicated jobs like we had in the past as manager of a painting company, organizer of a tech startup, small drug ring runner, a marketer, and an investor. The job at the builder's warehouse droned on, and we lived a conflicted existence between trying to figure out what we could do with ourselves while feeling like we could but shouldn't start our own company. All the while we were on fluctuating doses of medication, which left us with waves of symptoms.

We went through a year of processing our story and sharing with newfound friends, building up the courage to take control of our life and trying to really exert ourselves in the realm of career and just living a more suitable life. By the end of 2016, we had met Ivan who had offered us an additional job and we began to work alternating between the builder's warehouse and as a construction assistant.

We had been sharing our story and tails of visions and drug experiences with our friends, but when we began talking to Ivan about what we had been through, we gained an outlet for acceptance and understanding we never expected. Ivan is an amazing friend now who has had an amazingly fascinating life, and we learned from Ivan more and more to not judge a person by their looks.

Ivan is intelligent, open-minded, wise, talented, and human. He was also living a fairly isolated life with contact within his own small community of friends and family. As we got to know and work with Ivan, we came to know that he did not talk about his beliefs with everybody because he had not found a community that shared his vision of reality. Ivan saw life through spiritual eyes and lived in a world that seemed to not acknowledge and accept his lived experience. We shared this plight with Ivan, and it made us open up to talking about reality.

As we worked with Ivan over the winter, we began talking about our beliefs, "delusions," hallucinations, altered states, and perceptions of what truth was. We would continue to talk to Ivan about these topics in depth for years. The point is his acceptance about our beliefs helped validate our identity. In turn we began speaking to our friends more and more about our experiences that we previously felt had stigma attached.

At first, we identified with the stigma that we were mentally ill and therefore there was something wrong with us, but the more we shared, the more we were exposed to acknowledgement of our experience and acceptance by others. We had been so afraid to share our experiences and thoughts because we did not want to be labeled crazy. It turned out that our experience was actually interesting to a lot of people. We had human experiences.

As we worked and socialized, we began to desire more and more to move on from our past paralysis and isolation and plan for a future. So, we started to form plans to become a physical therapist. Physical therapy would allow us to fulfill our goals of making really good money and helping people. We just were not sure how to pay for school. We loosely decided we would start studying the material and figure out the rest later.

We made the drastic decision that we would pay for school by trying to join the military and use the GI Bill to pay for school. The only problem was that we couldn't use medication if we were going to join the military. We figured we could convince military shrinks that we were fit enough mentally to serve in the army national guard if we could manage going off medication.

Over the course of 2016, our medication had gone down many times and every time we reduced our meds, the symptoms seemed to be less and less severe. Our previous psychiatrist had been trying to get us off medication altogether, but we did not discuss our plan with our new psychiatrist and just decided to go completely off medication on the first day of 2017. We wouldn't be scheduled to meet with our psychiatrist for at least a month, and we were determined to join the army and prove that we were capable before we turned thirty-five and were no longer eligible to serve in the armed forces.

39 TRYING TO STOP MEDICATING

Years after our personal schism, in 2017, we still had not completely put ourselves back together. On the first day of the New Year, we went off medication completely. Through 2016 we had experimented three or four times with reducing medication to nothing over the course of weeks, and it seemed that every time we went down in dosage, it would be longer and longer until we were overwhelmed by symptoms of voices and visions. We felt like we had finally reached the point that we were ready for a big change. It is just that stopping medication turned out to not be the change we were ready for.

Over the course of January and February, we remember feeling very good and as time went by, our energy shot up. We became more sociable and creative. We became more adventurous and outspoken. It was like a veil was lifted, and we could be ourselves again. We heard voices when we went to bed, and as the weeks went on, voices slowly began to emerge from their long slumber.

By March we were having constant internal conversation with voices every day. Now this does not mean that we were in a conversation with voices; in fact, a lot of the time we were working or hanging out with friends or just doing the daily tasks of living and trying to avoid engaging voices, but that did not mean that the voices were quiet. The voices persisted and at night as we lay in bed, we saw fantastic images play like movies through our mind. Sometimes we could control the content, but the images always were changing and morphing from moment to moment. Nothing seemed fixed.

By the end of March, we were completely infatuated with voices. We ended up going up to New Hampshire to visit our brother's family, and we were so engrossed in conversation with our voices that we did not realize we were mentally developing codependence with the voices. We began listening intently to everything they were saying, and our thoughts began to engage in fantasies that involved taking a journey across the country. Essentially, we just wanted to leave our circumstances behind and be immersed in the world. As we stood in the kitchen of our brother's house looking out the window at the world we really wanted to explore, we made a sudden decision to leave.

We did not want any part of our circumstances. We were fed up with the long period of time it was taking to get back on our feet. We were tired of being isolated from the world, and we knew we were capable of a lot more than working a job at a builder's warehouse and of doing menial construction labor. Our frustration with the product of our life to that point in time was becoming the drive to move on. We were feeling alive like we had not in a long time, and so we decided to leave our brother's house and start walking. We did not say goodbye. We just walked by the kitchen, down the hall, out the door, and up the driveway.

We did not look back and we headed for the main road in an elated mood. It was the same path that we had tread naked many years before, only now we had the good sense to wear clothes, and this time we were not following any commands. We were doing this of our own accord, and we were having wonderful conversations with the voices about the possibilities that lie ahead. As we walked away from the house, we began playing games with the voices and horsing around.

When we reached the main road, we took a right and began thinking about the path we were going to walk and how we would get by. We figured we had a debit card and over $25,000 saved up from work and disability. We knew we could last on the road for a while but were unable to make concrete plans because the voices were flooding us with stimulus.

As we began walking down the main road, we do recall a strange event; we experienced walking getting very difficult, like our entire body got heavier. As we walked, we felt like we were fighting against something to leave. But as we continued down the road, we got used to the weight we were carrying and slowly the effects of the resistance began to pass, or we just got used to them.

We walked for hours and conversed with voices to pass the time. The topics and the mood of the voices would fluctuate and always come back to us, focusing on our need for the voices to help us if we were going to live with them. After a few hours of walking, this topic began to get rocky. We vacillated from convincing the voices all the reasons they should work with us to hearing a torrent of reasons they would never help us. As we walked without food or water, we began to grow irritable.

Eventually, we began speaking out loud to ourselves as we walked with only speeding cars to keep us company. We figured nobody could hear us, so it couldn't hurt. But soon, talking evolved to expressing more and more anger and frustration, until we were yelling at the top of our lungs at the voices for not being cooperative. This led us to start to rage at the world for all the bullshit and crap that had been thrown at us. We yelled about the injustices in the world and all of the unfair things. The whole time, we just walked and screamed our heads off, and traffic kept on passing us.

That's when a police cruiser pulled up and flagged us down. This is my favorite part of the story because when the police officers got out of the cruiser, they began to evaluate us and we did not stop yelling. Instead of yelling obscenities and acting like we were out of control, we began to very loudly explain who we were, what we were doing, all about our history, and the fact that we were very frustrated and just needed to be yelling right now. We were genuinely ourselves and yelled at the officers, until they lightened up and began to joke with us. They did ask for our parents' number, which was called. As we waited and yelled and were amiable with the officers, our father and brother were on their way to try and intervene.

When our father arrived, we did not stop yelling. We just explained that we needed to go, that we were reasonable, and they should let us go out into the world and just live. Really, nobody had any legal reason to get an ambulance or anything and have us committed, because we were being honest about everything but the voices. At that point, we were also amazed by how great it felt to vent, yell, and show how reasonable we were. Eventually, the cops relented and asked us not to yell so loud, and our brother and father went home. We were free to go, and we just continued on our walk, feeling triumphant. We yelled a bit more but had a great feeling as we left the spot where we had been stopped.

We eventually calmed down and made our way on a path that we knew south. We began planning to walk to the coast and then south along route 1, until we made it to Connecticut and eventually back home. We figured this could be a journey to test and mold us, but we did not have anything but the clothes on our back and it was March, so the weather was still quite cold. By coincidence, we walked by a camping store, so we went in and went on a $1500 shopping spree. We bought clothes, hiking gear, walking shoes, and a pack complete with sleeping bag. We figured we would just sleep in the woods and just deal with the weather as we went.

At the time when we were leaving the shop, our father brought our mother in the car after us to say goodbye. When my mother got there and we began talking to her, we recall experiencing having the physical feeling that there was something unnatural attached to our stomach. We tried to explain the feeling to our mother that this was the way we felt, like we had a disease or a growth or something growing in our being that we had to resolve. We don't know that she comprehended what was going on within us, but we tried to communicate, but ended up with a haphazard goodbye.

We left the shop and set out east down a road with no map, just road signs. It was about four in the afternoon and we continued to walk until it got dark and rainy. We continued to converse with voices and found ourselves walking near a school and a grocery market as the sun began to set. We went shopping and got a bunch of canned goods, a can opener, some vegetables, and some water. We walked over to the sports field next to the school and ate a very plain meal of cold canned beans and vegetables without any utensils. We then set up our sleeping bag on a plank of wood under the bleachers.

We were cold and soon found out that our sleeping bag did not have insulation on the bottom. It was meant to have a sleeping pad under it. We were cold and it was rainy, but we bundled up in every layer we had and eventually drifted off to sleep. We didn't dream and we don't know how long we slept, but we woke up in the darkness to one of the cooler experiences we have had. When we woke up, we were in a state of ecstasy and union with the world. We felt space folding in and around us, and we eventually got a chance to play with the folding sensation as it moved around us. Then, we felt like a flexible spirit or part of the world or ourselves wiggled free of us and sped off into the world as our ecstasy abated.

By the time our "hypnogogic hallucination" abated, we were wide awake and decided it must be morning, so we continued on our way. Unbeknownst to us, we had only slept for a few hours and it was not even midnight. We had no watch or phone, so there was no way to tell what time it was, and we were already quite overwhelmed by what was happening.

We ended up continuing to walk into the night until there were no cars on the road. We felt like the night would never end, and we were stuck in some type of limbo of darkness. We walked for a few miles, then made camp down in ditch twenty or thirty feet off the road in the woods. Down in the ditch, it was wet, but there was high ground to sleep on. It was raining and we were becoming miserable because all we wanted to do was sleep, but first we had to set up our sleeping bag again. We began having trouble remembering which pockets we had gear in, and it took us a long time to find our toothbrush to brush our teeth. We began to have cognitive difficulty, and we could not block out the voices.

We literally felt like we were mentally incapacitated or disabled as we rummaged through pockets in our pack over and over to try and locate our gear. We spent at least thirty minutes just trying to figure out where all our gear was, and that's when we realized that if we were having this much trouble now, then we were not capable of traveling for days or weeks. We don't recall when we decided to turn around exactly. We have memories of exploring a huge construction site on the side of the road for an hour and trying to hide in the woods from the rain. We even considered taking shelter in a shed we saw in somebody's yard to get out of the rain, but what really matters was that we decided to turn back. The fact was that we were not capable of functioning to the degree that we would need to make a trip like this and be safe.

We found ourselves walking back the way we had come and heading for our brother's house. It would take hours of walking in the pouring rain to get back near his house. Then, a Jeep pulled over and offered us a ride to wherever we were going. We remember being incredibly confused about the ride, and the man in the Jeep was incredibly friendly but talked during the whole ride and seemed to know where we were going. He also admitted that he had a fatal diagnosis. At that point, we were witnessing our mind fluctuate wildly between comprehending our situation and trying to understand if the man was talking metaphorically or literally, if he was really a part of us and our narrative, or if it was a coincidence of chaos that was bringing us back from our failed trip.

We knew that we had medication back in Connecticut left over that we needed, and by the time we got back to our brother's house, we were soaked to the bone, freezing, confused, and ready to go back to Connecticut. It was early the next day when we got back and our brother asked us what we wanted to do because our parents had left New Hampshire to go home already. Our brother offered to drive us home, and we accepted.

On the way home, we tried to nap and closed our eyes for most of the ride, but after a while, we kept experiencing the need to stop breathing. At one point when we held our breath, we had an experience that made us start hyperventilating. We knew we were working toward something, and we breathed frantically and rhythmically and sensed like we were getting closer and closer to something. Then, all of the sudden, we felt like our consciousness hit a physical wall or barrier. We knew we had experienced the sensation before, and we don't know what it meant, but the experience faded and we found ourselves hyperventilating and decided to stop.

We should mention that hyperventilating is involved in holotrophic breathing, which can induce a psychedelic transcendent altered state. Our brother did not think that we were OK, and he asked if he should bring us to a hospital. At that point, we just had given up and we said, "Sure," so we just played dead in our seat and went limp. As our brother drove to the hospital, every turn on the road seemed to be synchronized with a change in direction of our thought process. Eventually, we reached the hospital, and we were hauled out of the car by attendees as we played dead.

We were brought into the emergency room and were poked, prodded, and checked for vitals. We just let everything happen to us as the nurses and doctors brought us to a room and performed scans on us, gave us a catheter, gave us shots, and tried to revive us. At one point, we got a shot of something and our eyes rolled open. As we stared at the ceiling tiles, we could see amazing designs in a yellow highlight that was quickly destroyed by involuntary movements of our eyes. It was like our eyes were shaking off the vison, and every time our eyes jerked, it became harder and harder to see the glimpse of magic that we knew was there.

The doctors and nurses eventually left us alone, and we heard that our father had arrived. We listened as my father and brother talked of computers and business and technology. The whole time, we were trying to figure out if they were somehow referring to our life. We could draw fantastic parallels between what they said and our life, but our observations may have just been a desire for them to make some comment about what was happening to me, but they were more comfortable discussing computers than any type of worry for us.

We ended up just opening our eyes and coming to after a while. We acted like we had not just faked our unconsciousness, and everybody just seemed to move on like we had not done anything wrong. So, even now, we don't know if our father or brother had any idea that we were faking. We also don't know why we faked this. We just know that the voices were in a constant state of transformation and were coming and going as we entered the hospital, like something was happening to them. In the end, we were admitted to the psych ward. This would be the last time to date that we were admitted to a hospital, and in truth, it was probably the best experience in a psychiatric ward to date

40 ENGAGING MY MENTAL HEALTH

2017 held a positive experience with a psychiatric ward, which was much different than my last forced encounter. I didn't voluntarily enter the hospital in 2017, and as I described, I was in a bit of a pickle. However, I also knew that very clearly and for some reason, when I got to the ward, instead of resisting treatment and resisting the experience, I decided during my time in the ward to embrace what was happening. I decided I would commit to the healing process, because more than anything, I wanted to come back and be able to live.

I participated in every group. I spoke with patients, carefully began to talk. More importantly, I listened to other patients that were there for reasons like having experienced mania and overdosing on melatonin. I had a peculiar relationship with two very wonderful, young African American women and even ended up kissing one with consent in the ward away from prying eyes. I attended meetings, played games, did puzzles, and just tried to be where I was in life and accept that I needed medication or life would be unbearable and unmanageable at that time.

My stay lasted less than a week because I was responding to medication and I was actively participating in activities. I made friends that I would try and keep, but fail, but it was a lesson that every friendship can't exist the same way from one stage in life to another, and there are always opportunities available for growth if you are open and committed to healing. So, I ended up going back to life and getting discharged to a mildly interrupted life.

I had been working at the building warehouse and had missed a few days, and I had interrupted my work with Ivan as a contractor. I basically had just disappeared without explanation, and when I got back to work, I realized I wanted to make a change in life. I thought that I still wanted to walk around the country, so I decided to quit the builders warehouse because I had found myself there, but could not, in good conscience, see myself continuing there in the future. I talked to Ivan and he agreed to keep me on and even work some extra hours.

My plan was to take the extra time I had to start walking when I could. I figured I could walk for a day or two with a backpack whenever I had the time and still make my psychiatry appointments and still work in-between. But then, a strange reality began to set in as I started getting adjusted to my new medication regiment. The haloperidol that I take increased the reward stimulus in my brain and made it easier to feel satisfied and in a way that inhibited motivation. I feel satisfied by everyday activities and lose the motivation to make drastic changes, like walking and camping overnight alone on the open road whenever I could.

As I began adjusting to reality, I had a chance or two to get started to walk about and just did not initiate. I ended up doing a lot of wishful thinking and posturing about how I would make a change and create a future for myself. As I was living life, I also began seeing a psychiatrist that I had in the past at GBMHC, but now I also started seeing a social worker. When I went to see them, I made the decision to lay it all out on the table.

When I spoke with my psychiatrist and social worker, I told them my entire history from 2009 to 2017, a briefer example of what I described within this writing. Something had changed in me; I had found that there was power in sharing the truth of my experience and it felt good. It felt so good that I began looking for a job that I could do that wouldn't be as hard as getting a degree in physical therapy and something that I could do online.

I began searching for programs online and signed up for information from a few schools and found a program in clinical mental health. At about the same time, my psychiatrist and social worker were trying to find me placement with a permanent outpatient facility to help me find a psychiatrist at an outpatient clinic. They gave me a bunch of options, and I ended up finding out that I could go back to my old psychiatrist that had refused to treat me if I agreed to go to counseling. I also found out that I could go to any of a number of nonprofit organizations that provided psychiatry with a counseling component. Some had group therapy requirements and others had one-on-one counseling. At first I resisted, but I contacted an agency in Fairfield and agreed to attend counseling session, which was new to me.

At the same time, I began to pursue a clinical mental health master's program and started to apply to school. I didn't really quite comprehend what the job was or how it would work, but I knew that it would involve helping other people, which is what I wanted to pursue in life. When everything finally lined up and I started attending counseling and was accepted into a master's program that trained counselors, everything clicked. I started to attend counseling as I started to work toward becoming a counselor.

This was just another wonderful step in the right direction for a serious experience of healing in my life.

41 COUNSELING

I was raised in a family environment where we did not talk about our personal lives. We did not generally acknowledge any type of mental suffering of any kind that we saw in one another. I learned to compartmentalize my life and share with others where I could. But my family remained off limits to the intimate details of what I was usually going through. This is at odds to what I see as healthy functional family dynamics.

As I began to study counseling I got a very basic education about what counseling encapsulated. Basically, the point of a counselor was to facilitate a space where trust could be built in order to work towards self-realization, competence, and confidence. Counselors were not there to fix problems, their job was to create a nonjudgmental, congruent, and supportive environment. Then counselors could help develop resources and skills so that clients had the opportunity to feel like they could stand on their own, be seen, and be empowered to work toward personal development.

I was amazed that this profession and its mission existed in this world, but even more so I was amazed that I had never even considered counseling as a part of my life before. Attending counseling was an experience which reinforced my beliefs today in cultivating vulnerability and honesty, in relationships, in order to give others, the permission to share. Studying counseling while attending counseling made the entire experience interesting and immersive because I was living the benefits of what I was learning first hand. I had the opportunity to learn from example and see both sides of the isle when it came to being clinician and client.

I started studying counseling at the end of 2017 and worked diligently taking courses while attending weekly sessions with my counselor Amy. I worked in conjunction with my new psychiatrist to approach medication with an open mind. Right from the beginning I was very up front about the fact that I had been on and off medication and I would prefer to be on little as possible. My psychiatrist worked with me to change the medication when I asked and I kept her and Amy in the loop about every experience that I had worth noting.

I disclosed when I was hearing voices, how often, I talked about all of the face stealing, energetic experiences, synchronicities, visions, metaphorical and literal confusion, alternative realities. But mostly Amy created a space for me to come and talk about my experiences where I didn't have to worry about being committed for experiencing the unconscious bleed through that is considered symptoms of a disorder.

Over the course of months, we explored what happened to me in depth. I talked about drug use, friendships, relationships, the psychedelic experiences, and I not only told my story but I began to see it in a different light. By describing my story, I started to become not only the one that experienced the confusion, madness, highs, and lows, the visions, the secrecy, and the isolation, but I developed the ability to become a storyteller.

The more I explored my story and analyzed what had happened in an open forum, the more I began sharing with my friends around me about details I had glazed over. My story became something that I could take ownership of by telling different tails of run ins with the law, my antics and excess as a drug dealer, or my psychedelic adventures that actually turned out to be entertaining and intriguing stories to those around me.

As I explored my story I also started to talk to my classmates in my counseling program. I had the privilege of meeting a bunch of other students who had found their way to counseling through personal adversity of every kind. I started to see that those that sought healing for themselves often found their way to healing others through life experience. I began sharing stories with others and grew bolder and bolder about claiming my history as my own instead of viewing it as a shameful secret.

The entire time that I was talking to counselors and students I was working with Ivan as a contractor. But honestly Ivan was just as big an influence on me as everything else because Ivan would talk to me about subjects that pushed my limits of acceptance and allowed me to way in my experience vs. his experience with spirituality and purpose in life. Ivan also made space for me to really explore what had happened to me while he offered his own two cents about what I was going through and gave me support so that I felt heard.

My friends also allowed me to talk about my experiences which I am grateful for. I began talking to Dan and Antoni about my beliefs of the collective unconscious, spirituality, life, death, God, purpose, fate, time, and everything in-between. Antoni and Dan listened and made space for me.

Dan, Antoni, and Ivan showed that I was capable of friendship again and having fulfilling and loving relationships based on exploration and improvement of life.

Everything seemed to be going well. Voices were under control due to medication, and I took a new tactic with them. I stopped trying to control and manipulate them. For a time, I didn't try and teach them anything. I listened and interacted when I could, but I was focused on building a life where healing could be my focus.

Since everything was going well for the beginning of 2018, I began to take less medication in cooperation with my psychiatrist. The effect was that I slowly but surely was exposed to more voices over time. Then I began trying all kinds of techniques to calm and quiet the voices. I looked into meditation. I explored mindfulness. I tried exercise. I was managing to work, listen to voices, and have a social life.

Home life with my parents would ebb and flow. I kept trying to improve my relationship with my parents as I learned about counseling. The issues in my family became more and more blaring as I learned about supporting others, compassion, different theories of counseling, and listening techniques. I honestly used what I learned in counseling on friends and family and found that it worked to differing degrees.

I was happy although juggling all kinds of alternative perceptions, ideas, voices, work, friends, and family. Despite the fact that I was really living in quite a difficult way I was happy. I was not fulfilled but I was happy. Then I got into a relationship. I met Bethany a few times at a friend's place and then again at a party. At the party I decided I would like to get to know her better and we ended up planning a meet up which turned into a date.

I was upfront with Bethany from the beginning and told her about what I went through, my history, and my current regiment of psychiatry, medication, and counseling. Surprisingly she was not scared away and we started dating. So I was seeing a woman for the first time in seven years, working hard to study and make money, and socializing with people where I could share who I was. It turned out I actually had an interesting life when it came down to it.

42 JOURNALING

At about the time I started dating Bethany I had worked up enough confidence in myself and my storytelling ability to do something about what had happened to me. I decided to start journaling. And the floodgates opened. I discovered another avenue to process and gain ownership of what had happened to me. And when I wrote I never knew where I would end up but it always seemed fascinating to me. Writing allowed me to make connections that I couldn't with other people other than voices.

I should mention that I was listening to voices often and instead of arguing or fighting with them I started to co-author ideas with them. It was like the voices were an avenue to out of the box thinking because they approached problems differently and presented me with obstacles that I needed to think about from different perspectives to navigate. My voices began to inspire me to write and I started to come up with all kinds of ideas which I started to record.

In addition, the part of my life that I really started journaling about daily was my dreams. Every night I wake up early in the morning with memories from vivid fantastic dreams. I usually have at least three dreams a night if not more. Historically my dreams take me to faraway lands, impossible vistas, buildings of every type of time period and architecture, I have met countless beings of every kind both fantastical and conventional, I have flown, been drowned, fought in wars, played soccer, explored futuristic vistas, been in movies, watched countless visions bodiless, and even heard a prophesy while dreaming. The amazing part is that sometimes my voices are featured in my dreams and they seem to be embodied in characters in my dreams. At least they say so when I awake.

I started journaling in October of 2018 and including this memoir have since written over one thousand pages of entries, ideas, blog articles, experiences, and dreams down. Writing has been a way to develop ownership of my life through becoming an author. Not only can I tell the story orally, but now I am able to write about my ongoing experiences and the wisdom that they allow me to share.

43 CAREER?

At the end of 2018 at about the time I started dating Bethany I also finished up a course in career counseling. This course explored aptitudes and assessments that corresponded to the art of career counseling and helping clients find appropriate jobs. As I took this course the message was that I should really love the job that I did. However, I was not certain about counseling. I enjoyed the subject matter, but I couldn't imagine myself sitting with other people just listening to other people for forty hours a week. I had so many ideas for businesses and non-profits and I had really not fulfilled myself as an entrepreneur.

I also was coming down on medication and really wanted to see friends more because while taking classes I was restricted because I was working and taking classes full time. So, I decided to put classes on hold and do something creative for a change.

I contacted my friend Dan and asked him if he would like to start making music. Keep in mind Dan is a musical savant that plays at least seven instruments and had a makeshift recording studio in his basement. He had taken a hiatus from making music because he lost all the music he recently made. Dan also was supporting a family and didn't have a ton of time but we started to work on music in his basement.

The first time I went over to Dan's he gave me a demo of what he could do with the software he had and the music recordings he still had. Within ten minutes of listening to him I was fully experiencing music racing through my body, up my spine, and as Dan manipulated the controls to manipulate the music my body responded in turn with sensations and feelings that you would need to be played like an instrument to comprehend.

I was intimidated but I thought there was something there so Dan and I started to make music. So, I was writing, making music, spending time with friends, working, attending counseling, and dating. Things were really shaping up and only getting better as far as I could see. Exploring my life and revealing what happened to me had become normal. I was exploring creativity in multiple pursuits and I was hearing voices regularly. Life was good and only seemed like it could get better until my medication dropped so low that it stopped working.

44 A HICCUP

Everything seemed to be going well but voices were becoming more and more present in daily life. Eventually this became a problem. One weekend while I was home alone and Bethany was busy I sat at home listening to voices. They became so overwhelming that I found myself unable to stop them. I laid in bed for hours trying to block them out but nothing would work. I began hearing unintelligible voices in the basement talking to one another and had my standard voices non-stop trying to convince me to give up and just give into them.

I was so angry that I began to shout at the top of my lungs at them. I did this until I was exhausted and hopeless. In my desperation I made plans to go hiking and considered making a trek on the Appalachian trail. I was trying to plan a journey that would give me some relief from the voices, even though it had not worked in the past. I was trying familiar coping mechanisms to solve an impossible problem. So, after the weekend of torturous listening I gave in and took a relatively small dose of anti-psychotics.

The result was that the voices immediately calmed down. By the time my parents got home and I got back in touch with Bethany and friends, I was fine, but my confidence was shaken. I stopped writing for a time because I was discouraged that I couldn't go off medication and that I needed a pill to live. I felt like there was no escape from voices or the fate of surrender that I would eventually have to face if I went off medication.

I recovered and ended up having my medication upped by my psychiatrist and the urging of my counselor. They worked with me to encourage me to keep dosing myself in order to maintain my sanity. It was not a bad proposition; one of the side effects of being on lower doses of medication is that I am more perceptive, more expressive, more adventurous, and just about more of everything. Raising my dose slightly calmed me down and allowed me to refocus.

After a few months of calmer waters, I ended up breaking up with Bethany because she had some personal issues arise that couldn't survive the relationship. She told me she loved me and that we could still be friends but then texted me just about once since. I was disappointed that such a supportive and kind part of my life evaporated, but relationships change in life and I took it in stride.

By the beginning of March 2019, I was feeling free again, I was happy, still exploring music, writing again, working, socializing and trying desperately to connect with my family. Things weren't perfect, but some things were getting to their limit.

45 OUR IDENTITY EXPERIMENT

By April of 2019 I had processed a lot of my history through writing and storytelling. I was still going to counseling and processing through the many thoughts and ideas that came with analyzing the colorful unconscious bleed through that lower medication was allowing me to experience. I was beginning to realize that I was okay being a voice hearer. I started to feel as if I could openly acknowledge my voices and bring them into the world of conversation with others in a new way. I wanted my voices to be able to talk to other people and I wanted to serve as a medium.

The decision to try and act as a medium was prompted because essentially, I realized what a large role that voices were playing in my daily life. Voices had more interaction with me and knew every thought and every activity that I took. In a way the voices had a transparent view of my life and reality. It would be difficult for me to actually be deceptive to the voices unless I was in denial and believed in lies and then they still might even have a clue about the truth of what was going on with me.

The thing is since I felt like I was transparent to the voices, I wanted to become more transparent to the world and bring my voices to light so that they could be heard. I started to record my voices talking by typing on the computer and eventually wrote what they said. I loosely set time aside to record the, so that they could have the experience of being present in the world which they were only able to do vicariously through me.

Then I went a step further and I decided to identify as a collective human being. Instead of referring to myself as "I", I began to identify as "We". This was actually quite a difficult venture. I explained the change to my parents and got anger in return. Then I explained the change to my friends and I got acceptance. I started to explain to anybody that I came into contact with if they asked and otherwise I just used different pronouns to identify myself. It is actually present in this book where I started to refer to myself as "we" which may have caused some confusion. I felt like I should keep the content because it allowed me a different state pf mind.

I went on as a "we" for some time. When I started to acknowledge the voices by being a collective they actually became very quiet and I thought that I was doing something genuinely healthy because they faded into the background as I acknowledged their existence through practice. I was once gain very happy, I had free time and I decided to go back to school to continue my education. School was slated to started in June of 2019.

46 THE "WE" HICCUP

"We" began courses in family therapy and substance abuse therapy. "We" were excited as we began reading the material, so that we could see how it applied to our own symptoms and condition. "We" took the opportunity to reach out to our teachers and explain our identity to them in an effort to be transparent and share our identity. The result is that, as we explained to one of our teachers how we identify as a "we," they expressed their welcome to our new class and then directed us to a link that gave us information for mentally ill and disabled students.

So, I ended up trying to write my teacher that I was a whole self, clarifying that I am not mentally ill, and trying to explain in frustration that I was trying to just introduce myself and I was not looking for help about student resources for mentally ill or disabled students, which she, a well-certified doctor and counselor, just had accidentally given me the feeling that I was being judged as. Her reaction was pretty normal for your average person that really doesn't know how to keep from slipping up, and on one hand I don't fault her for her failure to recognize my e-mail. On the other hand, I found her reaction distasteful, and it led me to realize that if I wanted to start a conversation about schizophrenia and the inherent biases involved in the condition, this is one of my entry points.

I ended up withdrawing from my courses with the realization that if I were to explain my identity and my knowledge with the condition of schizophrenia while trying to learn the material in the courses and also work full-time, I would not have enough time to take care of myself and have a social life. On top of which, I have this writing that I have come to love dearly and has become a place of reflection and revelation, and it would have to be put on hold because, honestly, journaling my thoughts and ideas is an enormous effort that takes time and energy, which I would not have if I became completely emerged in schoolwork.

I would like to finish my work that I plan to publish and have written pages of dreams and observations I would like to describe and explain, to really show the benefit of journaling dreams and the insight that writing can have if a person takes the time to reflect and get a picture of themselves down on paper, so that others may actually gain some modicum of experience of others and get a foot into a shoe other than their own.

47 GOING TO THE HOSPITAL FOR A REALITY CHECK

After the day that I dropped out of school, the most telling event that happened is that I have been more honest and open with my friends about who I am and the vision of reality that I have and how I hope it can help reshape the world. I have not been met with any skepticism, but instead engagement and acceptance that I tried to bring home to my family. As a result, on the morning of June 2, the day I was to start painting my family home and work to help my family, I got up early, walked out to the living room, and saw my father sitting comfortably in his morning routine. I decided to ask him, "Hey, Dad, do you believe that reality is literal or metaphorical?"

His response was not what I expected, because instead of just having a casual and open conversation about a topic I believe to be an interesting and enthralling subject that is telling about reality and the learning that could be had from it, he became intensely upset and insulting. I don't remember what words were transacted, but I know I was not about to accept his reaction toward me, which is that of a dismissive and disgusted person that did not want any part of open honest discussion about an interesting topic. He was immensely uncomfortable, and I knew that I had struck upon an important topic and decided to pursue him and try and get him to actually engage with me.

Long story short, he became more and more upset as I beset him and became more passionate about the fact that I was just trying to connect with him. He fled from me, and I followed him desperately, trying to be myself and passionately pointing out that he couldn't even talk to me about a seemingly innocent subject that held a seriously upsetting reality for him. I knew there was something important about this subject, so I did not let up, and he threatened to call 911 and the police. He repeatedly told me contradictory things like "Get out of my face!" when he could not even look at me and his back was to me because he could not face his son.

I resolved that if he needed to call the police in order to get me to stop trying to connect with him and have a conversation, then he might as well do it. He called 911 and tried to talk to them, and I interrupted him and ensured the 911 people that this was a family matter and that my father was just completely denying me. I knew I was upsetting, but I was tired of not being able to express myself with my family and I am tired of their reaction to any form of deep communication, so I let my father call the police. Then, when he hung up, I stopped and went outside to wait for the police.

I was in my underwear and a robe, and I just waited outside for them to come. Two police cars and an ambulance arrived. The police officers came up and asked what was wrong, and I began to explain in detail what had transpired to the officers. I was reasonable and orderly, although incredibly passionate, and I hoped to convince the officers that everything was OK. But while I explained my side of the story, my father explained that I had a history, and so the police told me that the paramedics had to check me out.

Then, three paramedics approached and I engaged them in the same passionate way. They knew I was not a threat to them or my family, that I had not threatened anybody physical violence, and had not really done any harm other than making my father uncomfortable and the fact was that I felt he was utterly denying me. A discussion ensued, wherein the officers expressed that they needed me to get checked out. I began to open a discussion about what they knew about schizophrenia and they began to tell me a story that fit the typical biased view of my condition. I asked one of the paramedics named Kyle if he would like to talk about the topic, because, clearly, he seemed interested, but the officers and paramedics had their jobs to do and they became impatient with me. They were there to take me to be evaluated, which is the procedure in this case.

Mind you, there was no legal documentation that they provide showing their authority. There is no agreement that I ever made to give them authority over me. There were six of them and one of me, and they had taken the side of my father because he called in the fact that he was uncomfortable. He knew he was not in danger, but even so, he was so threatened that he decided to use my medical history in order to be free from his discomfort. I was willing to go through the process, but I was unwilling to cooperate with their show of force. I told them exactly how it would play out: (1) I would not consent to be taken to the hospital and be evaluated because I was completely sane and this was a family issue; (2) I would go to the hospital and be honest and open, and I would be released;

and (3) I would not cooperate with them and walk to the ambulance, so they would have to drag me because I knew I was beginning to annoy them and intimidate them even though there were six of them and one of me.

I told them they were threatening me and that I was acting like a cornered animal because they were giving me no true choice, and I felt as if my rights and freedom were being violated. They had no written authority or reasonable reason to actually take me in my robe and shorts at my most vulnerable away, and I was logical and reasonable with them. I couldn't even get officers to be direct with me because I would be talking to an officer and my mother would interrupt and then the officer would act like he was confused by the fact that I was trying to speak directly to him. In the end, I sat down in peaceful refusal to cooperate and they brought me to the ambulance.

I began to speak with Kyle, the paramedic that I had asked if he wanted to have a conversation about schizophrenia. I started to explain the stigma and medical mischaracterization of the condition as a disease, and the history of how the diagnosis developed. We discussed the implications of family relationships on the development of symptoms of schizophrenia, the correspondence of emotionally undeveloped families, and the prevalence of resulting symptom sufferers. He and I talked, and he told me that I was the first person that he encountered that actually knew what was happening and has the education to be able to talk to him. He acknowledged me and told me I was on to something with my desire to educate and talk about this, and we began to talk about who he was and how he got into his job.

In the end, we had a lovely open conversation, and by the time we arrived at the hospital, we were on friendly terms. He had told me about his personal life and how he became a paramedic. In the end, I thanked him for actually talking to me and holding to his word to discuss. After we were brought into the hospital, I heard him exclaim something like "He was actually a pretty cool dude" as he left. I had entered the waiting room for the ER early in the morning before it was busy. There was one other patient really waiting in the hall: an old couple with a concerned-looking wife. There was a woman at the entrance watching the door and a woman at the desk doing paperwork.

I started to talk to them in a good mood and they seemed happy to talk to me, but after a while, work resumed and I had to sit. A man approached from the registration and asked me to sign a form to register myself with the hospital, which I decided to read. First, I actually asked him if he knew what it was about and he didn't really have any clue. I asked the nurse if they knew what it was about, and they didn't seem to know what the registration form actually described. I even asked the woman at the front entrance if she knew what all the people that came in were consenting to, but nobody had any clue about what this document was for. There was nobody available to explain why I had to sign this, so I began reading the document aloud and it was hilarious.

The document they wanted me to sign made me consent that I was liable for all the expenses the hospital incurred, that I would pay regardless of my financial situation, and that if I didn't pay, I could apply for financial assistance to pay for the stay—a stay that I did not consent to. I went through the legal ramifications and the many paragraphs that explained how I was signing my rights away and that the hospital took no responsibility for a slew of negative outcomes of being a patient. As I read this, I laughed and continued to ask other people if they could believe that the hospital even had the right to sell anything important that they discovered in my DNA. I had to disclose information like if I had HIV, and they were allowed to sell that information and my DNA information to third parties and I would not be compensated.

The hospital literally wanted me to sign a paper that would give them the right to sell my very physical essence and make me responsible financially for my stay when I did not consent to be there. I did not sign the paper and then I had to wait to be evaluated. A man named Cliff came to me, after who knows how long, and he began to interview me. Once again, I explained to Cliff the situation and the fact that I was there because of an internal family dispute, and once again it began a discussion about mental health and became quite intellectual before he had to be pulled away. He seemed impressed, but he had to do his job. So, after waiting for almost five hours, he visited me over and over. At a certain point, I told him this was ridiculous and I just wanted to leave. He asked me to see the psychiatrist and be evaluated. He told me it wouldn't take long, which was a blatant lie, but he did not have the legal authority to discharge me, so I consented to waiting.

After being in my head for hours and just sitting and finally convincing the nurses to let me change into my clothes and actually appear a bit dignified, a woman came from the psych ward to escort me to be evaluated. I was brought down the hallway by a security guard and a woman, and I reached a set of doors, which had to be opened with an ID badge. At which point, I demanded to know what the procedure was, because I did not consent to being caged. The waiting area before being evaluated is essentially a series of cells, like a prison holding area. The walls are bare, the floors are cold and hard, and the area is devoid of any visual comfort other than the attendees.

I got into a bit of a tiff with the woman in charge because she did not have the time to actually talk about the process or what was going on in the hospital. She was clearly on a schedule and had no patience or time to actually explain what it was going to be like or honestly how long I would have to wait. I agreed to go into the room if she gave me something to do, because it was obvious she was upset at not being categorically obeyed. That is what the hospital wants: conformity and good behavior from people in crisis. People have to wait for hours in crisis with no treatment. People are left to suffer in their own heads and watched and kept in the dark about the procedure and the legal ramifications.

There is a lack of transparency in this system, and it is terrible for the people that must endure these conditions when they are in crisis. Perhaps, in some cases, patients may not be able to communicate, but that does not mean that transparency should be lost. There's a slew of other patients who are desperately trying to figure out what is happening while they feel completely powerless. This is a great metaphor for my experience with schizophrenia or hearing voices. I was basically given the choice to conform and follow the system without any sign of what to expect other than the medical opinion that I was diminished in my capability to comprehend. Patients are not treated as human beings, and the system does not meet the needs of those that rely on it.

In the psych evaluation, I had to wait additional hours. I passed the time listening to attendees, hearing that the psychiatrist or a nurse practitioner was busy and would be back in a short while, that the attendees would text her and she would definitely be back soon. The attendees chatted on their phones, talked to one another, and joked while people in front of them were isolated, alone, and suffering. They did not seem to be aware of the fact that the people in these cells were in a state of limbo and there was no real attempt to truly comfort these people beyond pleasantries and enforcement of rules.

Once again, patients in crisis were forced to wait and suffer in unengaging rooms with no real distraction from their condition, a reassurance that the doctor would eventually see them, and the expectation to behave and conform in a prison-like manner that we can only imagine is completely uncomfortable and lacking support for somebody in crisis.

It seems like the hospital's main treatment for people in an emergency is time because I continued to wait and wait. I eventually got paper and journaled about my experience. I even talked to my sister and my father on the phone. My father told me he loved me and we got interrupted by the woman who took down notes about our condition and interview us for basic information. So, before he could explain himself, I had to hang up on him because the woman that was starting the evaluation process told me she could come back later. I wanted to get this over with, so I just hung up on my father, which was probably the wrong choice.

I explained once again the situation to this woman, and every time I told my story, the family roots of dysfunction became more and more clear. This woman empathized with me as I got upset when I described that my father, the man I grew up with, idolized, and loved, was the man that couldn't deal with me and my truth. She said she only had a few minutes, but she stayed with me and empathized with me. She was friendly and open, and I think she knew I did not need to be where I was because she took extra time to stay with me. After she left, I spoke with the attendee on and off, sat, stretched, tried not to hear voices, or pay attention to a stream of recognition about connections in life and recognition of the connections I was experiencing in my environment that continue to bear fruit of evidence about the truth of reality.

When the nurse practitioner finally saw me, hours later, it was about three o'clock. She asked me more questions, and I explained again and again that I got emotional about the rejection that my family had for me. This woman was familiar with family therapy and told me that perhaps I was asking too much of my family and that perhaps they were not equipped to actually handle my truth or really actually acknowledge me directly. She advised me to take more medication and left to come back later and tell me that I could be discharged. She called my father and asked if it was OK if I went home, and I agreed, although he was concerned about my medication. She came back in and asked me if I would like her to ask him for a ride, and I said that would be fine. The nurse practitioner left again and came back and said that my father said he could give me a ride at five after he mowed the lawn. He was more concerned with mowing the lawn at that point, so that it would look good for the neighbors.

I told her I could just get a cab, that I had money and credit cards, and that I could just get my own ride instead of waiting to be discharged. Even that process took what seemed like a lifetime. By the time I left, I went back through the emergency room and saw that the couple I had seen when I first got there was still waiting to be seen. They had been there since before I was brought in, which was after 7 a.m. It was after 3 p.m. and they were still waiting with a line of patients in gurneys. This was incredibly sad and revealing about the inadequate facilities for emergencies.

I went home in a cab. When I got home, my father treated me like nothing had happened. He didn't really want to look at me and avoided any confrontation. It's not like he could say I love you to my face or tell me how he called my boss and broke down crying, or that he talked to my sister and told her that he wished he just told me that he loved me. It was like I was back in eighth grade hearing everything secondhand because nobody was comfortable with direct communication.

I had made an agreement the day before that I would watch my friend's house for ten days while he was gone. This house-sitting gig was supposed to start today, on the 3rd. In the morning, my dad had said he would take care of that task, but I had no intention or need to be admitted, so I came home and made arrangements to go to Ivan's house as planned. Just the day before, I had talked to Ivan and his wife and had to convince Ivan's wife that it was perfectly OK that I take care of her precious animals and pets and that I was reliable, and then this disaster happened. When I spoke to Ivan, his wife asked if I could bring a family member over with me just in case, and so I ended up going over to Ivan's house with my father and mother, in awkward silence, to go over the mundane tasks of taking care of a household that

I was put in the position where I had to prove my sanity to professionals, and my medical history allowed my father to be in a position to escalate a family dispute to a psychiatric facility because of the stigma attached to mental illness and the legal precedents and procedures that do not appropriately address the rights of people with a history or present symptoms and put people in crisis in a situation where they must obey, conform, and wait among all other things with no real treatment for hours because of the lack of available resources and the apparent lack of training for the medical staff to actually make the patients feel like they were actually human. To me, my experience of the hospital this time was eye-opening to the practice of making patients feel even more helpless, and the policies of the hospital only reinforce that fact.

Now, I do not believe that these problems are the fault of the people that are working in the facilities or the doctors or nurses because they all seemed completely lovely in their own way, but the system itself is the problem, and the system is reinforced by these people. The question becomes, why do these people come to accept the system instead of looking at how it could be better? And why do the powers that be feel comfortable with the way the system is, why do they treat patients like they do, and what are the hospital administrator's priorities? Do they even realize that if they changed their facilities, incorporated counselors and psychologists, added more psychiatrists, and made resource and transparency available for these human beings, the hospital could actually make a difference for humans instead of being concerned with saving a dollar?

Even the toilet paper in the facility was thinner than a sheet of paper. The only real comfort they seemed concerned with was giving patients a menu that was expansive and allowed for ordering off a vast menu that catered to all types of needs, diets, and promoted healthy eating. It seems like the hospital believed that people need nourishment. The question is, what nourishment do humans need as opposed to patients?

48 REACHING OUT

After I successfully navigated my trip to the hospital I found myself back at home. I ended up upping my meds which I was not excited about but I was hearing voices a lot and my comfort was not the priority. The priority seemed to be to satisfy the world around me. I needed to take medication so that I didn't become too honest or make anybody uncomfortable because my support didn't want me back in the hospital.

After the hospitalization I also stopped identifying as a "we" because I found the experience to be too difficult. If anything, there should be a pronoun for voice hearers to describe being part of a group or whole so that people are aware that we have parts that are not easily identifiable by just looking at us. I am certain this idea would not pass muster with all voice hearers, but for me saying that I am an individual is misleading because I am more of a part of a greater whole with access to a gateway that allows me to communicate and observe beyond what others consider normalcy.

As I came back to being an "I", I also started to look into other voice hearers experience. I didn't really ever talk to anybody else that had heard voices and I figured to better understand myself I ought to start looking for information about other voice hearers. I started to order books about voice hearers from Amazon. I read a whole bunch of stories about other people diagnosed with schizophrenia that had lifelong struggles and I was amazed that I hadn't considered other sufferers before then.

In effect I had approached a diagnosis of schizophrenia and voice hearing alone. I recalled being given a flyer for Hearing Voices Network groups years previously when I was hospitalized and I started to consider trying to meet other voice hearers. I started to look online and found that there was a CT HVN and there was a US HVN organization. I started to reach out to find out about groups.

The first three times I tried to attend groups the groups no longer existed, so I ended up getting in contact with the agency in CT that ran the CT HVN. They invited me for a public meeting at their headquarters and I ended up attending. Now I was looking for a community because I started to think I wasn't alone with my experience and I was discovering that there were a lot of people out there that had gone through the madness I had.

49 DIAGNOSIS?

I don't recall exactly when but I had an appointment with my psychiatrist before or around the time in which I visited the hospital briefly. One of the things that she wanted to discuss with me was my diagnosis. I was informed that I had been given the diagnosis of schizophrenia and that it was in question. I was told that she didn't know what I had exactly but she no longer though I had schizophrenia because I was dealing with my condition so well.

She told me that maybe I had mania with psychotic features, but at this point I was not really convinced that I had any disorder. The fact is that the medical model tried to label its patients in order to categorize us and make us more manageable. But the diagnosis they give us are dehumanizing and misleading. The consequence is that as the medical model tried to tell you what is wrong with you in a way it is trying to define you so that it can apply a protocol for a defined problem. The medical model tried to compensate for constellations of experiences by creating vague broad labels to try and group together sufferers so that it is easy to comprehend what a person is going through.

The truth is that the story of my life is how I started hearing voices. If I tell a doctor I have schizophrenia that doesn't do justice to the massive amount of experiences, madness, epiphanies, feeling, observations, ideas, and perceptions that are present in my or any other person's phenomenology. Boiling my life down to a diagnosis is really dehumanizing because it is removing the context of my life. And doctor's in my experience tend to focus less on history of life events and more on "problematic symptoms" which they try to alleviate chemically.

I have done a great deal of research on voice hearing over the past year and I have found that in the fifties schizophrenia was treated with talk therapy and considered a reaction of the unconscious mind trying to reorganize personality in order to transform life. Then in the eighties the focus became on the brain and chemistry and ever since then the medical model had been trying to chemically induce sanity.

Schizophrenia had been deemed a brain disease which is completely false because there is no evidence of it being so. Any evidence has to do with brain scans that showed differences in brain structure of patients with schizophrenia, but those patients had been on antipsychotics. There are actually a lot of studies which point to antipsychotics causing brain damage and even studies that say antipsychotic can hinder recovery in many cases and cause more problems with psychosis.

I have to deal with the fact that medication has become necessary because it has actually made me more likely to be psychotic without medication. That is a side effect that no doctor warned me about when I started taking medication. I doubt my psychiatrist acknowledges the dangers of antipsychotics and the dependency they create, but that is what the current medical system is doing. Turning patients into diagnosis which generate money.

50 TRAUMA

In current studies, a large percentage of those experiencing voices have been through trauma. I started to read about this as I continued researching hearing voices and the hearing voices movement which has been growing for the past thirty years.

It made me reconsider my own experience, but furthermore I was led by breadcrumbs to what may have contributed to my voices. When I attended a three-day retreat for hearing voices group facilitation I got to hand out with a lot people that were working to make the world a more humane and supportive place. Something happened on the morning of the third day where I had a dream which led to an unlocked memory and a connection between what happened in the past.

I realized that when I was a child around the age of ten it was about the time when the Berlin Wall had fallen and about the time we had begun bombing Bosnia. Reports of the war and chaos were all over the news. I can recall very vaguely thinking about war and not really being able to wrap my head around the suffering and death that human beings were causing one another. After all I was a human being and up until that point I had lived in a safe and secure world where all my needs were well met and I was allowed to be a child.

On some level I believe that I could not reconcile the world I was seeing around me and the reality that I was living with. I realized that there was a serious problem but couldn't do anything about it because I was a child and I did not believe that anybody would listen to a child telling the world we needed to stop harming one another. There was another way.

I cannot recall the chronology of my early voices and visions and I should mention that I did not include every experience I had in this work, but I do believe the visitation of the wise men and the first voices happened after I began struggling with the concept of war and what humans did to one another. Then I began to experience the snow plough dreams which may have been the unconscious pain I had to go through in order to prime myself to live in a reality which was permissible of violence toward our companions on this rock that we travel through the universe on.

After my initial experience with voices life went on and there seemed to be many revelations and epiphanies that accompanied my youth. I had gained knowledge about the extent of what humans were capable at a young age, but I still hadn't found the motivation to do anything about it. When I started to smoke marijuana and take psychedelics later in like I believe I was highly motivated to make a living but I was not focused on the primary problems of our world. I was concerned with money and success.

My second bout with voices was partially due to the madness that exists in our world. The sheer hypocrisy, confusion, contradiction, and incredible corruption that goes on in our world and makes our elaborate set of systems which support life go awry for so many human beings. My second bout of experimentation had a purpose, to prime myself for continuing to live in a world where humans can treat one another like they would treat objects. Where the system itself treats us to dehumanize our experience despite the fact that every lifeform carries its own reality around with it and that we are all the same and part the same unified experience of life.

Now the voices are most likely with me for life because my experience as a human is as a symptom bearer for everything I have seen and perceived. One thing that is not commonly accepted about those that go through psychosis is the phenomenology of perception and the truths that we get exposed to which really sum up the madness of the world. I am lucky enough to be able to identify a lot of the mechanisms and information that I perceived so that I can translate my experience into digestible information for the masses. That isn't everybody's cup of tea.

Those that experience trauma and then go through unconscious bleed through like visions, spiritual awakening, or uncommon perceptions are like society's canaries that are put down in the mines where coal was extracted from the earth. We needed coal to power our world and the canaries were so sensitive that they would perish if there was poison in the air. Like the canaries we sensitive souls are the ones that are presenting with symptoms of something greater than ourselves. A toxic condition in our external realities that society is not addressing because of its all-consuming complex nature.

Psychosis, voice hearing, and other very human experiences can relate information about the systems that govern us, dictate our lives, and the madness that people learn to ignore in everyday life. Not everybody is lucky enough to be able to turn a blind eye to the problems we see, and some of us are compelled to manifest the problems we see to our core. So, I will most likely hear voices for the rest of my life.

My personal experience is that my voices have taken over the world in a way with the madness that I taught them. They exist in this world and around me constantly reminding me of the reality I live in and the chaotic nature of what I perceive in this world. The personal narrative that I constantly am revisiting is what am I doing to heal the wounds of the world and make it so the madness can be understood, useful, and let me live with myself.

51 RECOVERY

The recovery rate of schizophrenia is above fifty percent. It is probably higher than even doctors would imagine because I was told I would have a serious condition for the rest of my life and I should expect to work very little and consider disability.

People that recover from schizophrenia, psychosis, or spiritual emergency are also reported to have a better life afterward. Honestly the last three years have had me feeling happier, more engaged, and grateful then the rest of my life. These are facts that people don't equate with conditions of madness.

I went to the meeting about the HVN and ended up meeting with other voice hearers and I am currently working on getting involved in the Hearing Voices Movement. I have trained to become a group facilitator and I am in the process of setting up groups in my area.

While working for Ivan I started to get more and more confident in my work to the point that Ivan told me I was ready. I ended up starting my own business a few months ago and I have been busy doing home improvements to make end meet while writing and slowly developing my next steps.

I still hear voices and I would like to share them with others, along with my thoughts and wisdom, directly from the well of observation of my own experience. I have some pretty wild insights, but they are mostly geared toward expanding and explaining about what the variety human experience includes. I am writing a blog and working on a podcast among other pursuits. I am back to my entrepreneurial ways.

I acknowledge that I am still in recovery and am working toward making healing a way of life. I hope that if you read this book you saw the arc of a very human story. And saw the story of Winning Back Life.

Please visit my web page to see what's new at www.chancelove.blog

ABOUT THE AUTHOR

Chance Love is a writer looking to encourage others to share their hidden experiences. With his story he hopes to show that vulnerability and honesty can combine to create a compelling narrative geared towards healing. Chance Love is building a community around existing in the open and acknowledging the brilliance of humanity. He lives in rural Connecticut and spends time writing and studying in-between running a home improvement company. If you would like to contact Chance Love feel free to e-mail him at chanceloveadvocacy@gmail.com

Made in the USA
Middletown, DE
24 April 2020